1858

PICKLED

Vegetables ◆ *Fruits* ◆ *Roots* ◆ *More*

PICKLED

Vegetables ◆ Fruits ◆ Roots ◆ More

PRESERVING A WORLD OF TASTES AND TRADITIONS

◆

LUCY NORRIS

photographs by ELIZABETH WATT

Stewart, Tabori & Chang
New York

This book is dedicated to my grandmothers,
Frances Patton and Mary Norris

Published in 2003 by
Stewart, Tabori & Chang
A Company of La Martiniére Groupe
115 West 18th Street, New York, NY 10011

Export Sales to all countries except
Canada, France, and French-speaking Switzerland:
Thames and Hudson Ltd.
181A High Holborn, London WC1V 7QX
England

Library of Congress Cataloging-in-Publication Data
Norris, Lucy.
Pickled / by Lucy Norris
p. cm.
Includes bibliography references and index
ISBN 1-58479-277-9
1. Pickles. 2. Canning and preserving. I. Title

TX805 .N67 2003
641.4'6–dc21   200219827

Edited by Marisa Bulzone
and Trudi Bartow
Designed by Nina Barnett
Graphic Production by Alexis Mentor

The text of this book was composed in Cheltenham.
Printed in China by C & C Offset

10 9 8 7 6 5 4 3 2 1
First Printing

Contents

INTRODUCTION

In 1998 I uprooted my life. I left my job in Dallas and moved to New York City with a renewed dedication to finish my education. While working on my B.A. at New York University, I got more than a degree. I discovered my passion for food from an anthropological perspective—specifically how people express their values and identities through the creation of food and feasting. I began to see all the different ways that food has subconsciously influenced my feelings and decisions. As I came to appreciate and think about what I ate, I did so with more humility. And although I've always liked cooking and being in the kitchen—it has always been one part science experiment and one part craft—I began to notice the beauty and simplicity in growing, cooking, and sharing foodways with others. All this newfound passion led me to search for like-minded people—a quest that ultimately brought me to the NY Food Museum.

After stumbling onto their website, I became a volunteer intern to work on their *History of the Federal School Lunch Program* exhibit. A year later, convinced that I could make a difference, I offered to coordinate an oral history research project documenting New York City pickle history for the museum's first annual New York International Pickle Day. As I began to interview New Yorkers about local pickle history, I was surprised by how many people shared their personal stories or told me about a favorite homemade pickle. Many of the stories and memories had little to do with New York. As the project expanded, I widened my focus and began collecting stories and recipes from people throughout the United States, with different ethnic and regional identities, who wanted to preserve (or at least share) their personal memories and food traditions. This book began as a result of that research.

Many of the recipes included on these pages have a special history. Some emerged from fond recollections of the "good old days" here in America, where, for example, a grandfather prized his tomato patch in New Jersey and pickled "the pink ones" in his 5-gallon crock. Other recipes recall lifetimes a world away. Tina Yam recalls with longing the bittersweet memories of a time when neighbors casually strolled through her village back in the Philippines—a harmonious place wiped out almost thirty years ago by violence and corruption—sharing meals and telling stories. To Renuka Potluri (whose daughter claims she makes the best pickles in the world) recreating a family recipe for pickled mango transports her, as if by magic, to her family's mango orchard in India.

The recipes are important; they represent more than just food: They are a link to another human experience. Pickles, in this case, are a kind of time capsule through which we explore and learn. When we preserve food, we preserve a memory. By preserving food traditions, we pay tribute to the people and places that shaped who we are today.

A Little Pickle History

Pickles, like many preserved foods, are an important part of diets throughout the world. Their history can be traced back to ancient Egypt, where it is believed Cleopatra ate pickled foods as part of her beauty regimen. Before refrigeration and electricity, pickling food saved it from spoilage and provided sustenance during harsh winters. Without pickles, world exploration would not have been possible. Pickles provided something rich in vitamins for people to eat alongside staple foods, but they are also pleasing to the palate. In Asia and parts of Eastern Europe, pickles remain an important part of daily meals and snacks even today.

Pickles come in so many varieties; through the years they've been a supermarket staple. Photo courtesy of Pickle Packers International.

Pickles have gone in and out of fashion in the United States, where many fear their high sodium content and have excluded them completely from their diets. Some of the recipes in this book have very little salt: Try Groysman's Fresh Pickles with Black Currant Leaves (page 48) and Madge Kho's Pickled Shrimp (page 145), both low in sodium. I would advise anyone who enjoys pickles to eat them, but in moderation. As with any food, too much of a good thing is probably too much. But no matter when or where pickles are eaten, they are a healthy alternative to many modern snack or junk foods. Today we don't have to preserve foods at home because of the variety of commercially available products, but making homemade pickles, like anything you cook yourself, gives you total control of what you eat. Considering the excesses of commercially made products, this is a rarely enjoyed advantage.

Still, there are commercially made pickles that we all love and enjoy. We can thank the American pickle industry for this. I've included personal reminiscences and historic photographs of pickle packers and makers of other traditional ethnic foods. They share fascinating stories about how they started in the pickle business, what it was like, and how it's changed.

A Pickle by Any Other Name

Pickles are more than just cucumbers—although many people simply refuse to call a pickled food a pickle if it isn't a cucumber spear. Some go so far as to say that if it's not kosher, it's not a pickle! Some of the recipes in this book may not seem like pickles to you, but to the people who created them, they certainly are. In fact, Jacqueline Newman's Mixed Pickle (page 114), which calls for cellophane noodles, could easily have been described as pasta salad. However, the vegetables in this dish are clearly pickled: After a few days in the refrigerator, they become more flavorful, the mustard gets intensely hot, and the vegetables keep their crisp pre-pickled texture.

Using some sort of liquid brine—a salt, sugar, vinegar, and spice combination—is common to almost all pickling. The general differences lie in the climate and geography of a place, and the available foods and spices, all of which affect food choices and storage. Throughout the world, there are people who like their pickles salty and spicy, while others prefer them sweet. Almost everyone prefers a crunchy, firm pickle—and I'm not just talking about cucumbers. Whether they're made from beets, okra, herring, lemons, carrots, cabbage, or cantaloupe, hardly anyone likes a soggy pickle. In addition to standard brined pickles, recipes for fermented foods, such as sauerkraut and kimchi—a fermented vegetable "pickle" that's a staple in the Korean diet—are included in this book. Most South Asian pickle recipes call for a plethora of rich spices, combined with primary oils, citrus juice, and pickling salt, but use very little vinegar or added salt. And according to Tuhin Dutta, a New York–based tandoori chef who shares two family recipes here, just about everything gets pickled in India.

You may find your favorite pickles missing from this book. Although I've collected more than eighty recipes, they cover only those portions of the world that are somewhat familiar to me. But I've provided a wide range of techniques and methods that should give you some basic tools and insight to create pickle recipes of your own.

Pickle Your Own Tradition

The ongoing exchange between cultures in the United States has revitalized the American culinary landscape, resulting in a vast new cornucopia of color, texture, aroma, and taste. I hope you will see a reflection of some of that cross-cultural energy in this book, and that it will inspire you, the home cook, to preserve your own pickling traditions, create new ones, or help revive the art of pickling in your own home and community.

Safe Pickling

To avoid preserving food contaminants (specifically botulism and e.coli) along with your pickles, you will need to know a little about the risks. The following section on the mechanics of pickling describes the fermentation process and optimum conditions for pickling. After that, basic equipment—from crocks to jars to pickle presses—is reviewed, along with hot-water baths and other sterilization and sealing techniques.

In addition to this general information, if you have specific questions related to food safety and sanitation, please see the bibliography on page 154 for many good sources. Regardless of your pickling or canning experience, please familiarize yourself with these essentials before getting started. Pickling, like all cooking, requires some preparation and organization. If you are organized before you turn on the fire, your experience will probably be a good one.

Always be sure to use a clean, dry work surface, and prioritize sanitation whenever you are handling food and cooking equipment. Most of the recipes in this book can be stored in the refrigerator in either a nonreactive bowl or a pickling crock. However, when the jars need to be sterilized before they're filled, then processed and sealed in a hot-water bath afterward, I have indicated this in the recipe, and detailed directions appear on pages 12 to 14.

Correct processing ensures that your pickles stay fresh and safe to eat, whether or not you plan to store them in a cupboard or mail them to your friends and family. Generally you only have to process pickled items that are going to be stored for months in mason jars to develop their flavors fully. This can take time, so be patient if your pickles aren't very flavorful the day you make them.

Pickle Mechanics

Pickling, especially when looked at from a global perspective, can mean several things. When a brine, typically made of saltwater and spices or salt alone, is used, the pickles are fermented. This is a process by which safe bacteria already in the food breaks apart sugars to create acid (mainly lactic acid). Moderate acid production helps to preserve the food for an extended period. Too much acid, however, halts the fermentation process. Salt controls the fermentation process, fosters the growth of good bacteria, and draws out excess, often bitter liquid from the food. Salt also firms the texture of pickles and concentrates and balances a host of herbaceous, sweet, and spicy flavors. Without salt, fermentation progresses too quickly and the pickle *never* sours enough.

Pickles brined in vinegar typically do not ferment, but vinegar isn't added to pickles just for flavor. Vinegar or citrus juice discourages the growth of harmful microorganisms in pickles.

Getting Started:

BASIC EQUIPMENT AND PROCEDURES

Pickling and canning equipment has changed little in the last century. To get started, you will need glass jars, caps, and lids. Some of the pickles in this book will require a traditional hot-water bath: This means that the jars must be processed in boiling water for a specific length of time after they are sealed (see pages 12–14 for instructions). Others, sometimes called "refrigerated pickles," can simply be put in a nonreactive bowl or container, covered, and stored in the refrigerator until they're ready to eat.

If you do not have a boiling-water canner, you can make one by placing a clean, raised rack in a large stockpot. If jars have direct contact with the bottom of the pot they will become too hot and may burst. You should also make sure the stockpot is wide and tall enough so that boiling water will cover the jars completely by 1 to 2 inches.

If you are just learning how to can (as this method of processing is often called), keep it simple and go with mason jars. Named after John L. Mason who patented their clever design in 1858, these jars, with their vacuum caps and screw-on lids, are easy to find and totally effective at keeping contaminants out of your pickles. Kerr and Ball brands have been the most common jars for years; now they are both manufactured by the Alltrista/Jarden Corporation.

For the recipes in this book, you will need pint, quart, and gallon jars. You can find both jars and lids in most hardware stores or see Sources, pages 151–152. Buy by the case if you have the storage room; it should be much cheaper than buying individual jars—and I have rarely if ever made just one jar of pickles.

Regular lids and caps fit both pint- and quart-sized jars. However, lids can be easily bent when prying open a sealed jar. Since they are relatively cheap, it's safest to use new ones each time. The rule of thumb: Make sure your jars and lids are in perfect condition. That means no cracks or flaws in the glass, and no bent or punctured caps or lids.

Basic Equipment

Canner or extra-large stockpot: for processing jars in a hot-water bath; the canner should be equipped with a wire basket, or use a wire rack to raise the jar in a stock pot.

Mason jars, caps, and screw-on lids: see details, above.

Measuring cups and spoons: for both liquid and dry ingredients.

Wide-mouthed jar funnel: this funnel has a relatively wide opening, which ensures a clean transfer of ingredients to the jar.

Bubble freer: a plastic knife or clean chopstick is the perfect nonreactive tool for getting rid of air pockets in your pickles.

Jar lifter: these are special tongs made for lifting jars in and out of hot water.

Small kitchen tongs: for lifting screw-on lids in and out of hot water.

Clean dish towels: always keep several on hand for wiping around jar lids after sealing and as hot pads.

Extra large bowls with lids and colanders: for mixing ingredients, rinsing, draining, or letting pickles stand overnight.

Knives: a chefs' knife and paring knives are a must.

Food processor: nice for quick chopping, mincing, or pulverizing ingredients, but not essential.

Mortar and pestle: for making spice pastes.

Coffee grinder: specifically used for grinding spices.

Cheesecloth and cotton twine: to make a spice bag in which whole and ground spices can be boiled.

Ladle: for scooping hot pickles into jars.

Specialty jars and lids: for adding frill to ordinary jars, you can purchase decorative caps and old-fashioned green glass jars. If you prefer jars with sealed wire bails and glass lids, you will make an equally good pickle with a little more effort. See Sources, pages 151–152, for suppliers who sell these items.

Sterilizing and Processing

At least one hour before you plan to start your pickles, collect your canning equipment and inspect it for flaws and cleanliness. If you have a dishwasher, you can simply clean the jars by washing and then leaving them in the washer on the dry heat setting. This way, they will be fully cleaned and stay warm. According to Linda Ziedrich, author of *The Joy of Pickling,* and several other people I interviewed, this is a safe method cleaning, but please note the jars are not sterile. As long as you intend to process your pickle in 180°F bath for at least 10 minutes to process, they should be fine—those bad bacteria will be dead. However, the Alltrista Company and the USDA do not recommend this practice, although they speak on the side of caution.

If you prefer the old-fashioned method, turn your oven temperature to warm or 200°F. Rinse out your canner and clean your utensils. After inspecting your jars and lids, place the jars on their sides in your canner or extra-large stockpot, and then fill the canner with hot tap water. Enlist a friend if you need help to carefully transfer the canner to your stovetop. (My canner takes up almost half of the surface area on my kitchen stove.) Turn the heat to medium-high and cover the pot. It will begin to boil in about a half hour. Return the water to a simmer and, using kitchen tongs, carefully grab the jars, tilt them so the water escapes back into the pot, and lift them out of the water one by one. (Keep the water at a simmer until you're ready to replace the empty jars with full ones.) Place the hot jars in a large roasting pan and transfer them to the preheated oven until you are ready to use them.

Sterilizing the Screw-On Lids and Vacuum Caps Fill a medium saucepan with water and bring it to a boil. Lower to a simmer and then add the screw-on bands. Do *not* boil the vacuum caps: Put them in a separate bowl (like a cereal bowl) and, once the water from the saucepan comes to a boil, you can ladle just enough water over the caps to cover them. Let the lids and caps sit in the hot water until you are ready to use them.

Filling and Sealing the Jars Carefully remove the jars from the dishwasher or oven, using an oven mitt if necessary. Bring the hot jars and your stockpot full of hot pickles to a flat surface where there's plenty of room to work. Place the clean, wide-mouthed funnel over a jar and then ladle your pickles into the jar, allowing for head-space as indicated in the recipe. Remove the funnel and carefully insert the bubble freer (do not stir) to break up any air pockets that could potentially harbor the growth of nasty bacteria.

Once your jars are filled, remove a cap from the hot water with a fork or small tongs and place it, centered, over the mouth of the jar. Remove a screw-on lid from the hot water and screw the band on firmly, but make sure it's not too tight. You want some exhaust air to be able to escape during the processing. Fill and cap the rest of the jars.

Processing the Jars in a Hot-Water Bath Use your jar lifter to carefully place each capped jar in the wire basket of the canner. Lower the basket down into the still sim-mering water so that each jar is completely submerged—the water should clear the jars by 1 to 2 inches. (If you are using an extra-large stockpot, use the jar lifter to place the sealed jars on the wire rack at the bottom of the pot, making sure that the jars are completely submerged.) Leave the jars in the simmering water (160°–180°F) for the specified length of time, which is 10 to 15 minutes in most cases.

Once processed, carefully lift the jars with the jar lifter and transfer them to rest on a dry towel spread over a flat surface; make sure they are out of the way of traffic. Gently wipe the water from the lids, being careful not to jostle the contents too much. As the jars cool, the pressure inside will pull the caps down in their centers to create a vacuum seal. You may hear a pinging sound as the seal is formed. The first time I did this, I was concerned that I didn't hear the ping—don't worry! You'll know if the cap is properly sealed because the center will be completely depressed and won't give to the touch.

Let the jars sit for about 10 hours until they cool fully to room temperature. The jars are ready to store. You should remove the screw bands but if mailing, I usually replace them to keep the seal in place. Re-process any unsealed jars or store them in the refrigerator.

The Altrista Company, makers of Ball and Kerr jars, sells complete starter kits like this one, with everything needed for canning. Photo courtesy of Alltrista.

Vintage Pickling Equipment

Moving beyond your everyday Ball and Kerr jars, historical pickle equipment, such as wooden barrels and antique earthenware crocks, are a pleasure to collect and use.

Wooden pickle barrels have been used to make pickles for centuries. In Japan the *okeyasan*, or cooper, was an artisan who would fashion wood and bamboo into everything from small pickle barrels to towering soy sauce vats. In Poland giant 5-foot-tall wooden barrels stored sauerkraut during the long cold winters. Slightly smaller barrels or crocks were used for cucumber or tomato pickles.

Commercial pickle companies in North America began replacing the old wooden barrels with new leak-proof plastic barrels during the 1970s. Sure, wooden barrels are historically interesting and many traditionalists will argue that pickles made in wooden barrel were more flavorful, but to those in the industry, there are quite a few practical advantages to using plastic. Full wooden barrels weighed 600 to 650 pounds each and they were prone to leaks that promoted bacteria growth in the wood. During shipping, the pickling liquid had to be carefully watched and often refilled. After a few uses, wooden barrels became quite odorous and the bands tended to rust. They would have to be washed multiple times or thrown out—a costly decision.

The bottom line, according to Tim Baker, owner of Guss' Pickles, is "wooden barrels were an expensive pain in the neck! Full plastic barrels weigh about 500 pounds. They never leak or rust and can be easily rinsed and reused. They cost less to ship or replace if necessary. They are more sanitary and last longer. What's not to like?"

Large wooden barrels were often used by commercial picklers. Photo courtesy of Pickle Packers International.

Earthenware or stoneware pickling crocks In North America, many of us have at least seen a photograph of the multi-gallon earthenware or stoneware crocks once commonly used for home pickling. Before refrigeration, these crocks could be stored in cool root cellars away from contact with heat or light, which protects them from over fermentation or cooking. The mouth of the lid was often covered with gauze or linen and tied with a string to keep pests from creeping in. A plate was set over the mouth and a heavy can or stone kept it all in place. You can find earthenware crocks at antique shops and occasionally, if you are lucky, at flea markets and garage sales or buy them new (see Sources, pages 151–152). Many people who contributed crock-pickle recipes to this book inherited their crocks from family members or found them through a stroke of good luck, just like you can.

Pickle crocks generally hold at least 1 gallon. I have seen smaller ones, but all the crock-pickle recipes in this book has been written to yield about that amount. If you want to make more pickles, simply multiply. Before you use the crock, make sure it is completely clean and free of cracks.

Victorian pickle casters In the Victorian era, prior to refrigeration, condiments such as sweet pickles and East Indian relishes or chutneys were very popular in both England and the United States. Traditionally one or two beautiful glass or crystal containers were filled with homemade pickles and set in silver dishes. They were passed politely at the dining table from guest to guest—just as salsas and ketchups are today. Victorian pickle casters are now an antique collector's item. Some are true works of art engraved with idyllic nature scenes, rimmed in silver, or with gold-plated handles and sometimes serving tongs or pickle forks attached.

Kimchi vessels An important fall tradition in Korea is gathering people together to make huge quantities of *kimjang kimch'i*. During this important social event, the kimchi is prepared and layered into celadon-glazed earthenware or wooden vases. Once the vessels are filled and covered, they are buried underground and left to ferment for at least a month in order to preserve the flavor throughout the winter months.

To make more common, everyday kimchi, it is not necessary to bury the kimchi or even use a specific kimchi pot—although there are some beautiful ones (see Sources, pages 151–152). Nonreactive glass bowls or earthenware pickle crocks will work just as well and take up less space in the refrigerator. If you have access to one, a Korean food retailer will sell every ingredient necessary for making kimchi. And if you are ever in Seoul, visit the Kimchi Field Museum which has an extensive exhibit on the history and art of Korea's most well-known and important food, and even a hands-on kimchi-making workshop.

Japanese pickle press The *tsukemonoki* or pickle press is an indispensable kitchen tool in Japanese kitchens. Once the vegetables are salted, the platform is screwed down, pressing moisture out and away from the vegetables. Pickle presses are inexpensive and can be purchased from Japanese food retailers or from a variety of online stores. (see Sources, pages 151–152.)

Know Your Ingredients

As with cooking and baking, your pickles will be best if you always use the freshest, most seasonal produce, as well as fresh meat, eggs, herbs, and spices. Make sure your vegetables and fruits are not bruised or spoiled, and never use hard, pink supermarket tomatoes. Ideally foods should come straight from your garden, but if you are like me, you depend on what's available at the farmers' market or local produce stands. If so, choose vegetables and fruits that are in season and look freshest for your pickles. Some of the recipes in this book call for semi-ripe or even green produce.

According to the Penzeys Spices catalog, "Old spices never go bad, they just fade away." Spices that have graced the presence of your spice cabinet for years may be safe, but they'll taste like sawdust. Buy only small quantities, and since spices generally lose their flavor within a few months, keep them in airtight containers with the lids tightly sealed or in Ziploc bags with the air pressed out of them before closing. Keeping spices airtight also prevents bug infestation.

Buying spices in bulk is only a good deal if you plan to use a lot of spices and your bulk supplier regularly rotates the supply of the kind of spice you are buying. Put your senses to work and judge by smelling the bulk supply before buying. If you aren't sure if the spices are fresh, ask the clerk when they last filled the bulk bin.

Below are helpful descriptions of common and uncommon ingredients used in the recipes in this book, along with information about use, availability, and storage. See Sources, pages 151–152, for possible suppliers.

Ajwain or Ajowan also known as caromseed or lovage is a spice used in many Indian and Pakistani dishes. The seeds are found in spice catalogs or at South Asian food stores. It has the aroma of sharp, piquant thyme and looks like tiny caraway seeds. Ajwain is also eaten to control bowel disorders.

Alum, crystals of potassium aluminum sulfate, is often called for in older recipes and was once widely used for keeping pickles crunchy. Aluminum is the active ingredient in alum and can be toxic if large quantities are eaten over time. There are less potentially harmful methods for ensuring a crisp pickle, but if you want to make pickles the old-fashioned way, you can purchase food-grade alum from your pharmacist.

Asafoetida is a member of the fennel family, long used as a spice and for its medicinal properties. A hard resinous gum, it is sold most frequently as a fine yellow powder. When cooked, it adds an onionlike flavor. Asafoetida should be kept tightly sealed for storage, as it has a pungent odor that will permeate other foods.

Black currant, cherry, and grape leaves impart a unique flavor to pickles, but their primary purpose is to help stabilize a crunchy texture. Use fresh clean leaves for pickles. If you don't grow them in your own garden ask local berry farms or wineries to reserve some leaves for you during the season. Grape leaves used for recipes in this book should be very tender early summer leaves that are green on both sides.

Black cardamom pods have a smokier flavor than the better-known green pods commonly used in South Asian and Middle Eastern fare. You'd be hard pressed to find the pods at your local supermarket, but they are sold through mail order and online spice catalogs (see Sources, pages 151–152).

***Bu chu jun* or Chinese chive** is a cross between a chive and a scallion: Flatter than a scallion and almost completely green. Korean *bu chu jun* is slightly smaller than the Chinese variety but the flavors are almost the same. You can buy seeds online if you want to grow your own (see Sources, pages 151–152), or purchase it fresh at Korean and Chinese produce markets.

Chinese rice wine is wine bottled especially for cooking. It is made from rice and contains salt. You can find this easily in Chinese grocery stores.

Cinnamon buds are the small dried berries of the Chinese cassia tree; they resemble cloves, but have the flavor and aroma of cinnamon bark. In fact, fresh aromatic cinnamon bark is an acceptable substitution, since the buds are more difficult to find and are somewhat more expensive.

Coarse pickling salt or kosher salt should be used whenever salt is required in these recipes, unless otherwise indicated. They do not contain the additives dextrose, sodium bicarbonate, and yellow prussiate of soda found in all iodized table salts. Additive-rich salt will make your pickle brine dull and cloudy and also will affect the taste.

Curry leaves, a main ingredient in Madras curry powder, can be bought fresh or dried, although fresh is more flavorful.

Da-dae-ki is a seasoned paste made with equal parts sugar, minced scallions, crushed garlic, grated fresh ginger, Korean red pepper powder (or cayenne), red pepper flakes, and enough dark sesame oil to form a thick paste. Korean cooks usually mix their own fresh, but it is also commercially made and available in some Korean groceries. Recipes for *Da-dae-ki* vary according to the cook's preference.

Fish sauce is made from salt, fish, and water. Asian fish sauces are sold in bottles and used in many recipes from salad dressings to noodle dishes. Look for bottles that haven't been sitting on the shelf too long. Fish sauce grows more pungent with age and contributes a similar "hint of fish" taste to Southeast Asian and Chinese dishes as anchovies do to southern Italian dishes.

Green mango and green papaya True green mango is a green-fleshed, firm, and bitter mango. It may be hard to find in most cities, but South Asian or Southeast Asian produce carriers stock them seasonally or get them on special order. Do not use unripe yellow mango for these recipes—it is not firm or bitter enough to hold up to the concentration of salt, spices, and oil. For substitutions try sour Granny Smith apples or crabapples instead. True green papayas are firm and have white meat. They can be found in Asian grocery stores, but if none are available, green cabbage is a better substitute than unripe fruit.

Horseradish is a root vegetable that is used widely in sauces and dressings. A little fresh horseradish root is a natural way to add a lot of flavor to pickles. It also helps maintain crunch. It can be found in most supermarket produce sections. Avoid using processed horseradish.

Illustration courtesy of Pickle Packers International.

Jaggery or palm sugar is a coarse, dark, unrefined sugar. It can be found in Southwest Indian or Asian stores in two forms: A honeylike liquid or a cakelike solid.

Kelp is a popular dark-green sea vegetable added to many Japanese-inspired dishes for flavor and nutrients. Kelp is typically dried in long hard strips and sold in plastic bags. It can be found in health food stores and in the ethnic food aisles of some supermarkets.

Lime (calcium hydroxide) is an ingredient found in older pickle recipes. Lime makes pickles firm. Commercial pickle products often contain some sort of calcium salts, which are found in lime, to improve the texture of their products.

Mace blade is a spice that is stronger than nutmeg, similar to cloves. Mace blades were once a common ingredient in soups, pickles, and meat dishes. You will often find the ground version in stores today. Blades can be purchased from spice catalogs (see Sources, pages 151–152) or from some baking supply shops. They look like amber-colored paint chips.

Mustard seeds are the seeds of the mustard plant. When they are ground, they become a powder. This is what table mustard is made from. Most Western recipes call for white seeds. Most South Asians prefer the toasty kick of brown mustard seeds. They can be found in spice catalogs (see Sources, pages 151–152) or South Asian grocery stores.

Mustard oil is an ingredient commonly found in Indian-style recipes. Mustard oil contains erucic acid and the USDA requires it to be labeled for "external use only" due to associations between erucic acid (also in canola oil and prepared mustard products) and cardiac lesions, but people in India have eaten it for centuries. Use only the amount of mustard called for. Mustard-flavored oils are acceptable substitutes if the risks concern you.

Nigella or kalonji, is a spice found in Indian and Pakastani dishes. It is also known as black onion, black caraway, and black cumin seed, although it is not botanically related to any of them, instead being the seed of the flower *Nigella sativa*. It can be purchased from South Asian grocery stores.

Pickling spice is a combination of spices commercially mixed to add spice to brined pickles. If you intend to make many pickles that call for pickling spice, it would be economically wise to mix your own. Typical ingredients in commercially packaged pickling spice include, but are certainly not limited to, allspice, white mustard seeds, cloves, cinnamon, dill seed, cracked bay leaves, peppercorns, and coriander. I have also heard of someone mistakenly adding taco seasoning to their pickles and they turned out delicious. Be creative!

Sesame paste and oil are both products of pounded sesame seeds. The brown oil is extracted from sesame seeds and has a toasty flavor. Chinese sesame pastes differ in flavor from Middle Eastern–style tahini pastes. Chinese sesame oil is darker than sesame oil most often found in American grocery stores, although the darker oil is becoming more common these days, and is the type preferred for use with the recipes in this book.

Shiso leaves are the leaves of the beefsteak plant—not to be confused with beefsteak tomatoes—or perilla plant, a member of the mint family. The plants can be grown in flowerpots or in an herb garden. I found them sold in small bunches at my local greenmarket for a dollar a bunch. The leaves can be either deep purple or green, and when snipped and mixed with other foods, their clean herbaceous flavor really shines through.

Sichuan peppercorns or fagara are not peppercorns at all, but the dried berries of the prickly ash or fagara. They impart a distinct "peppery" flavor to many Sichuan-style dishes known to be on the spicy side. They can be purchased from online spice catalogs (see Sources, pages 151–152), in specialty food shops, and Asian markets.

Tamarind pulp is the pulp of ripe tamarind fruit and can be found in brick and syrup forms. Both are available in South, Southeast Asian or Latin American groceries. According to folklore, tamarind pulp is used to treat nausea, flatulence, indigestion, and constipation. Tamarind is sweet, tart, and refreshing in taste. The bricks are usually 7 ounces.

Turmeric is a common antiseptic and an important ingredient in South Asian recipes. It puts the yellow color in curry powders. It is widely available in ground form. Whole root turmeric can be found in specialty spice catalogs (see Sources, pages 151–152) and South Asian grocery stores.

Vinegars Stock your cupboard with the following varieties to meet your pickling needs.

Black vinegar, found in Chinese food stores, is black, syrupy, and somewhat sweet. It is similar to balsamic vinegar and is made from a combination of rice and possibly other grains and malt.

Cider vinegar is made from fermented apples. This is one of the most common vinegars in North America and is also used frequently in pickling. It is inexpensive and widely available.

Red wine vinegar is made by fermenting red wine. Even if you make homemade red wine vinegar from leftover wine, I recommend that you use commercially made vinegar for pickling, unless otherwise indicated in the recipe. Homemade wine vinegar is too strong.

White wine vinegar is made from white wine and is common in recipes for French *cornichons au cru.* Again, please use a store-bought variety instead of homemade.

White vinegar is distilled vinegar made from vegetables. The most general-purpose and inexpensive vinegar available in North America, it is used extensively in pickling.

"WHAT ELSE WOULD YOU EXPECT TO SEE BETWEEN TWO SANDWICH BOARDS?"

Illustration courtesy of
Pickle Packers International.

CHAPTER ONE

Cucumbers

IF YOU'VE EVER GROWN YOUR OWN CUCUMBER PATCH, YOU ARE familiar with the dilemma of what to do with so many cucumbers. They really aren't very good cooked (summer squash already fill that role), so pickling is simply the best way to use these huge cucumber harvests.

Cucumbers come in many varieties. Different kinds of cucumber seeds can be purchased by mail order or from online seed catalogs. There are basically three types of cucumbers: slicing, pickling, and bush. Cucumbers are quite porous, and because they are almost all water, low in calories. Half a small cucumber with the peel on contains roughly 5 calories. The green peel, which is left on for many recipes, may taste somewhat bitter, depending on the variety.

In this chapter, you will find recipes that call for the semiseedless English cucumber (also known as hothouse cucumber), the Kirby, and the standard burpless supermarket cucumber, as well as the more exotic Japanese or *kyuri* cucumber, the Korean summer hero, and the elegant Persian cucumber.

These pickle recipes are time-honored family treasures from people who have preserved family traditions along with their pickles. They range from very basic to fairly difficult. Some call for sugar, some hot pepper, while others contain fresh dill; the Japanese shiozuke recipe (page 34) contains only cucumber and salt. You will see that the cucumber is the quintessential pickling vegetable, not just in the States, but all over the world.

Previous spread: Glad's Pickles (page 60) and Young Choi's O-I Kimchi (page 35) are shown, along with an array of varietal cucumbers suitable for pickling.
Above: Illustration courtsey of Pickle Packers International.

$\mathcal{T}$o me, summer means the aroma of my grandma's hot, Texas kitchen, the scent of carnations, roses, tomatoes, and cucumbers, drinking water from the garden hose, and the sound of the screen door slamming. I imagine myself in my grandma's small kitchen, which is filled with the steam of mason jars sterilizing in a big pot, surrounded by bushel baskets of tomatoes, cucumbers, and spices. My mom and grandma are chatting over a white, enameled pan of just-picked green beans and a plastic bucket full of colorful discards created by their paring-knife wands.

Sometimes I was given the task of paring green beans for canning or washing cucumbers for pickling. Handling hot canning liquids, funnels, tongs, jars, and lids was left to the adults. I knew this was serious business, and to my youthful eyes, it looked like an experiment in a science laboratory. While the women toiled over the cauldrons, I was busy scribbling my name on the chalkboard, or more likely, outside climbing a tree, eating blackberries off the bush, or looking at the neighbor's pet rabbit.

Grandma Patton died in 1996 after about six long years battling Alzheimer's disease. I have a box of recipe cards given to me when her house was cleaned out. Some of the recipes are from homemaking magazines and others were cut from the newspaper, but I realized that not all of

Grandma Patton (Frances Williams) in the late 1920s. Photo courtesy of Lucy Norris.

Grandma's best recipes were included. My aunt, Judy Lowther, who farms in Ohio north of Columbus, shared a lot of recipes with my grandmother and my mother over the years, some of which came from her mother-in-law, a good cook and a baker who even sold her homemade cakes and candy. Among the family favorites that follow, the bread-and-butter, dill, and mustard pickle recipes originated with Aunt Judy's mother-in-law.

Unfortunately rainwater is not as pure as it once was, so I would caution anyone who does not have a good rainwater filtration system to use distilled water instead. Aunt Judy tells me that they also used well water "back in the day," which added a mineral taste to the pickles.

This is the only recipe in the book that calls for cinnamon buds (see page 18). The freshest, most aromatic cinnamon bark you can find is a good substitute. Plan ahead. This recipe takes a full two weeks from start to finish.

SWEET CROCK PICKLES WITH RAINWATER

MAKES 1 GALLON

1 gallon cold tap water
4 cups coarse salt (kosher or
   pickling)
75 medium-sized Kirby cucumbers,
   about 17 pounds, scrubbed,
   halved lengthwise, and cut into
   chunks or thin slices
1 gallon boiling water
1 gallon clear, fresh rainwater or
   distilled water
1 tablespoon alum powder (see
   page 17)
3 quarts distilled white vinegar
24 cups (12 pounds) sugar
2 tablespoons cinnamon buds,
   or 2 to 3 pieces cinnamon bark
2 tablespoons celery seed

Combine the cold tap water and salt to make a brine. Put the cucumbers in a pickle crock, pour the brine over them to cover, and let stand for 1 week at room temperature.

Pour off the brine and replace with the unsalted, boiling water to cover; let stand for 12 hours or overnight. The next morning, pour off the unsalted water. Mix the rainwater with the alum and pour it over the cucumbers; let stand for 12 hours or overnight.

The next morning, drain the cucumbers in a colander. In a large, nonreactive pot, combine the vinegar, 6 cups (3 pounds) of the sugar, cinnamon buds, and celery seed. Bring to a boil over medium-high heat, about 15 to 20 minutes, until a syrup forms, and then pour that syrup over the pickles.

Cover the crock with a plate, then a clean dish towel, and secure it with a weight (like a brick or large can of tomato juice). For the next three mornings, pour off some of the syrup and add 3 more cups of sugar (otherwise the syrup will become too watery). The sweet pickles are ready to eat after the fifth morning, after the last addition of sugar has sat for a day.

Refrigerate them in the crock or store the crock in a cool, dark place, again covering it with a plate and dish towel secured with a weight.

These bread-and-butter pickles are ones my family is very fond of. I think my grandmother varied the recipe a little by adding whole white mustard seeds for extra texture and flavor.

BREAD-AND-BUTTER PICKLES

MAKES 4 QUARTS AND 1 PINT

28 to 30 medium-sized Kirby cucumbers, about 7 pounds, scrubbed then cut into ⅛-inch-thick slices
1½ cups coarse salt (kosher or pickling)
6 cups distilled white vinegar
3 cups sugar
1 tablespoon celery seed
1 tablespoon powdered mustard
1 tablespoon turmeric
9 onions, peeled and thinly sliced (optional)

Mix the cucumber slices with the salt in a large, nonreactive bowl. Put a plate directly on top of the cucumbers and let them sit for 12 hours or overnight at room temperature.

The next morning, drain the cucumbers in a colander and rinse them several times under cold running water. Transfer them to a large, nonreactive pot.

In another nonreactive pot, mix together the vinegar, sugar, celery seed, mustard, turmeric, and onions, if desired, to create a syrup. Cook over medium heat, stirring constantly, for about 5 minutes or until the solids have dissolved.

Pour the brine over the cucumbers and bring to a simmer over medium heat; simmer for 15 to 20 minutes to allow the water from the cucumbers to be absorbed and the liquid reduces back to a syrup.

In the meantime, sterilize the jars and lids according to the directions on pages 12–14. Divide the pickles and brine between the jars, screw on the lids, and process the jars in a hot-water bath for 10 to 15 minutes to seal. Let cool before storing in a cupboard for 1 week before eating. Sealed, they will keep for up to 6 months.

DILL PICKLES

MAKES 3 PINTS

1 cup distilled white vinegar
3 cups water
½ cup coarse salt (kosher or
  pickling)
8 to 10 medium-sized Kirby
  cucumbers, about 1 pound,
  scrubbed and left whole
3 sprigs fresh dill, or 1½ teaspoons
  dill seed
½ red bell pepper, stems and seeds
  removed, cut into 3 strips

In a nonreactive pot, mix together
the vinegar, water, and salt. Bring to
a boil over medium-high heat, stirring until the salt dissolves.

In the meantime, sterilize the
jars and lids according to the directions on pages 12–14. Pack the
quart-sized jars with the cucumbers
and add equal portions of dill and
red pepper to each jar.

Pour the boiling brine over the
cucumbers leaving about 1 inch free
at the top of the jar. Screw the lids
and process in a hot-water bath for
10 to 15 minutes to seal. For the flavors to fully develop, store the jars
in a cupboard for about 3 weeks.
Once opened they can be stored in
a refrigerator for 6 months. Sealed,
they will keep for 1 year.

My aunt thinks these may be the pickles I remember snacking on as a child—
and I do remember them fondly. My grandmother kept a gallon earthenware
crock of these in her refrigerator. She made them from the small cucumbers she
grew in her garden.

MUSTARD PICKLES

MAKES 4 PINTS

27 to 29 small Kirby cucumbers,
  about 7 pounds, each slightly
  larger than a man's thumb, or
  14 to 16 medium-large Kirby
  cucumbers, scrubbed
8 cups water
4 cups distilled white vinegar
¼ cup coarse salt (kosher or
  pickling)
2 teaspoons powdered mustard or
  prepared yellow mustard
¼ teaspoon saccharin, like
  Sweet 'n Low
¼ cup sugar

Put the cucumbers in a large, non-reactive bowl or pickling crock, pour unsalted boiling water over the cucumbers to cover, and let stand at room temperature for 12 hours or overnight.

The next morning, sterilize the jars and lids according to the directions on pages 12–14. In a nonreactive bowl, mix together the vinegar, salt, mustard, saccharin, and sugar to make the brine; whisking thoroughly to eliminate clumps.

Drain the cucumbers in a colander, then pack them in the pint-sized jars. Divide the brine equally between the jars to cover the cucumbers, screw on the lids, then process the jars in a hot-water bath for 10 to 15 minutes to seal. Store for about 1 week before eating. Unsealed, these pickles will stay good for 3 months if refrigerated; sealed, they will keep for up to 1 year.

This is another recipe given to me by my aunt. I sent a quart of these sweet pickles to my father in Texas and he said they were so good he ate almost half the jar in one sitting. He describes them as being unusually mild and softer on the palate than commercially made sweet pickles.

Be patient when making this recipe. You may think you need to add vinegar to your brine, but as the cucumbers simmer, they will continue to release water and create more brine. In fact, you will probably end up with slightly more brine than you need.

SWEET PICKLES

MAKES 5 PINTS

2 cups distilled white vinegar
2 cups sugar
2 cups dark brown sugar, loosely packed
2 tablespoons coarse salt (kosher or pickling)
3 tablespoons pickling spice, tied in a cheesecloth
25 to 30 ripe medium-sized Kirby cucumbers, about 6 pounds, scrubbed and cut in half sliced lengthwise

In a large, nonreactive pot, combine the vinegar, sugar, brown sugar, and salt. Add the spice bag and bring to a boil over high heat. Add the cucumbers, return the mixture to a boil, then reduce the heat to a simmer and cook until the cucumber halves are tender, 1½ to 2 hours.

In the meantime, sterilize the pint-sized jars according to the directions on pages 12–14. Transfer the mixture to the jars, making sure the brine completely covers the pickles, while leaving ¼ inch free at the top of the jars. Screw on the lids and process in a hot-water bath for 10 minutes to seal. Let cool.

Eat immediately or store in the cupboard for up to 12 months. Refrigerate after opening.

acqueline Newman grew up in New York City with easy access to the foods of her very close friends in Chinatown. She is now the editor of *Flavor and Fortune,* a Chinese food magazine published by the Institute for the Advancement of the Science and Art of Chinese Cuisine. At a young age, she was introduced to many types of Chinese pickles.

"The Chinese pickle recipes I've contributed (see pages 72, 87, 97, 114, 115, and 135) are those I remember eating as a child in Chinese homes and restaurants in New York City in the 1940s and 1950s. They are typical of Chinese pickled foods, and reminiscent of those I ate as a child and foods that Chinese eat today. Chinese pickles are made quickly and with a plethora of ingredients."

The recipe below may surprise you. It is not very salty or vinegary but somewhat spicy, although the sesame paste keeps it mellow. I use a cup of this pickle over cold soba noodles flavored with soy sauce and ginger. It makes for a very appetizing dish, especially on a hot summer day.

QUICK-CHILLED CUCUMBER PICKLES

MAKES 2 ½ SMALL SERVINGS

1 English cucumber, 1 pound, scrubbed, cut in half lengthwise, and thinly sliced
2 tablespoons Chinese sesame paste mixed with 2 tablespoons iced black tea
½ teaspoon coarse salt (kosher or pickling)
1 tablespoon toasted sesame seeds
4 to 5 Sichuan peppercorns, crushed
½ teaspoon minced garlic
1 teaspoon dark sesame oil
3 to 4 sprigs fresh cilantro

Mix together all the ingredients except the cucumber and cilantro in a nonreactive bowl. Add the cucumber slices and gently stir again to coat. Cover and refrigerate this mixture for an hour or two. Remove from the refrigerator and drain in a colander for 3 to 5 minutes (you will lose some of the dressing), then transfer to a serving platter. Top with the cilantro sprigs and serve.

***P*ickles are very popular in Japan,** where they come in many varieties, from very hot to mild and sweet. They are often eaten at mealtime to aid in digestion. Because they make you salivate, they are an important part of the Japanese-influenced macrobiotic diet. Some Japanese pickles require much attention and patience, while others are very simple to make, such as this recipe from the Asia Society for *shiozuke*, which makes a cool and tasty accompaniment for rice.

If you do not have a pickle press (see page 16), a good alternative is to put all the ingredients in a large, nonreactive bowl, cover with a smaller plate that fits inside the bowl, and weigh it down with a heavy object (like a stone or can of soup).

SHIOZUKE
(Salt-Cured Japanese Cucumbers)

MAKES 4 TO 6 SMALL SERVINGS

3 *kyuri* (Japanese cucumbers), scrubbed and cut into ½-inch-thick rounds
3 teaspoons coarse salt (kosher or pickling)

Place the cucumbers in a pickle press, add 1 teaspoon of the salt, and mix well using your hand. Add another teaspoon of the salt and mix again. Add the third and final teaspoon of salt and mix well. Clamp on the top of the pickle press, screw down the platform until it presses tightly on the top layer of cucumbers, and leave under pressure for about 10 hours to extract excess liquid.

Remove the pickles from the press and transfer to a colander; rinse well to remove all the salt, then pat dry with paper towels and serve. These salt pickles should last 1 week or more if refrigerated.

Variation: Along with the salt, you can also mix in 8 to 10 fresh shiso leaves (see page 21) that have been stacked and snipped into strips with scissors.

34

*A*lthough *I always think of kimchi* as simply Korean pickles, it actually is the result of fermentation rather than brining. There are literally hundreds of kimchi types—possibly as many recipes as there are people who make it. You can totally change your kimchi's taste and texture by simply omitting one ingredient or adding another. I prefer hot and spicy, complex foods, and kimchi has become one of my favorites.

Young S. Choi, owner of Woo Lae Oak restaurant in Manhattan's Soho, serves several recipes of kimchi that reflect both her French culinary training and her Korean heritage (see her recipe for napa cabbage kimchi on page 75 and radish Kimchi on page 88). You can find kimchi pots with lids in Korean markets, or you can make and store kimchi in earthenware crocks, glass jars, or other nonreactive containers. The result will be the same.

YOUNG CHOI'S O-I KIMCHI
(Stuffed Cucumber Kimchi)

MAKES ABOUT 5 QUARTS, OR ENOUGH TO FILL ONE 1-GALLON CROCK

20 Korean summer hero or Persian cucumbers or *kyuri* (Japanese cucumbers), scrubbed and cut in half lengthwise (see Note)
1 small daikon radish, peeled and minced
¾ cup minced white onion
¾ cup chopped watercress, about half a bunch
¾ cup chopped *bu chu jun* (Chinese chives, see page 18), about half a bunch
2 scallions, chopped
½ cup coarse salt (kosher or pickling)
½ tablespoon saccharin, like Sweet 'n Low
½ cup cayenne pepper or red pepper powder
⅓ cup *da-dae-ki* (see page 19)
1½ tablespoon minced garlic
1½ tablespoon minced ginger

In a large, nonreactive bowl, combine the water and ½ cup salt and soak the cucumbers for 30 minutes. Drain the cucumbers in a colander, cut off the ends of each cucumber, and with a knife or spoon, remove the seeds. (This hollow area will make room for the stuffing.)

Mix the rest of the vegetables in a large bowl, then add the seasonings and mix well. Stuff each cucumber half with the mixture and stack them upright in quart-sized jars or an earthenware crock. Cover and allow it to sit at room temperature for about 24 hours, then chill and serve.

Note: Since kyuri *are twice as long as the 10- to 12-inch Persians, cut them in half widthwise as well.*

The Pickle People is a family-run pickle company owned by Eddie and Lee Ann Jacobian of West Hempstead, Long Island. I first tasted their pickles at a Thunderbird powwow in Queens, New York, where they sold individual pickles from their Pickle Mobile and packed quarts for attendees to take home. When I returned to my apartment that afternoon, I realized I had lost my keys. I ended up on my front porch snacking on the Pickle People's Fabulous Cajun Pickles while waiting for help.

Eddie grew up in a pickling family. His Turkish grandfather made a mixed vegetable pickle from cauliflower, cabbage, celery, and carrots. Eddie's mother, Alice Akparian, remembers its salty-vinegary brine, but unfortunately her father passed away before the recipe was written down.

It seemed only natural for Eddie to continue the pickling tradition. "We started small in a shop in West Hempstead," Lee Ann explains. Slowly they built a following and, through word of mouth, the business grew. "Over time, nearby restaurant owners ordered pickles, then they had friends or cousins who owned restaurants, and before we knew it, a wholesale route developed. Today we deliver to diners, delis, restaurants, and even country clubs. Growing up, my husband became familiar with many different spices, which he incorporates into different kinds of pickles. I guess it's a kind of pickle evolution! Here we are today, twenty-two years later, still in West Hempstead and still pickling."

FABULOUS CAJUN PICKLES

MAKES 4 QUARTS

1 cup coarse salt (kosher or
   pickling)
¼ cup distilled white vinegar
1 gallon cold water
1 tablespoon Cajun seasoning
1 tablespoon chili powder
½ tablespoon cayenne pepper
1 tablespoon Italian seasoning

½ tablespoon ground cumin
1½ tablespoons pickling spice
½ tablespoon black peppercorns
1 head garlic, peeled and minced
50 small Kirby cucumbers, each
   about the size of an index finger
2 jalapeño peppers, thinly sliced
¼ white onion, sliced
10 cherry peppers, quartered

In a large, nonreactive bowl, combine the salt, vinegar, and cold water to create the brine, and stir until the salt is completely dissolved. Add the Cajun seasoning, chili powder, cayenne, Italian seasoning, cumin, pickling spice, peppercorns, and garlic; stir and set aside.

Sterilize the quart-sized jars according to the directions on pages 12–14, and pack the cucumbers and equal parts jalapeño, onion, and cherry peppers into them. Pour the spiced brine over the cucumber mixture until fully covered. Screw on the lids and let ferment at room temperature for 3 days. Refrigerate for another 5 days and they are ready to eat. They will keep for up to 3 months, refrigerated.

———

*J*ulian *Ezstergalyos of Portland,* Oregon, makes the best sun pickles. It's one of the few Hungarian traditions remaining in his family. "You never see this recipe in Hungarian cookbooks, either," says his wife, Theresa, suggesting that the recipe may have been adapted after traveling from Hungary to America.

"This is a special pickle which is often made in Hungary. Because Papa [as she calls Julian] came from Hungary, it's one of the many recipes I had to master. We have always called them sun pickles, as it works best when the jar is placed in a sunny spot outdoors. Also you need to use fresh cucumbers, so summer is the time to make them."

This is a naturally fermented pickle, using no vinegar or canning process, so sun pickles aren't made in large quantities to store away in your pantry. They are tasty, easy to make, and so different from ordinary dill pickles.

(continued on page 40)

Jean's Appetizing

AN INTERVIEW WITH EVELYN CASSIDY

Evelyn Cassidy's parents opened Jean's Appetizing in Bensonhurst, Brooklyn, on the same street as Marine Market, later called Krasne Brothers, and then White Rose. To Evelyn's knowledge, it was the first supermarket chain in New York City and her parents wanted to be close to it. When Marine Market became Krasne Brothers, her parents started looking for a private

Evelyn's mom and dad. Photo courtesy of Evelyn Cassidy.

store on the same block. A kosher butcher approached them about sharing a shop right next door.

The new location was good for managing customer traffic because the butcher would close his shop from about two o'clock on Friday until Monday morning, while the big day at Appetizing was Saturday. In the morning, they sold an abundance of bagels and lox and whitefish. At first Evelyn's parents were working seven days a week, but it got to be too much, so they cut back to half a day on Sunday, and eventually closing the shop completely on Sundays. That part of Bensonhurst was mainly Jewish, but there was a big Italian area down the street from Marine Park, recalls Evelyn.

Evelyn has a sister six years older than she who worked weekends at the shop. Since she was older, her sister learned how to handle the knives. She knew how to slice the lox, sometimes very thin depending on the likes of the

customer. Evelyn wasn't allowed to use the knives because she was the baby—
she would do the little things.

When Evelyn was nine or ten, she began working summers and holidays to
help her parents. "I'd sit outside with the pickles in the summer selling small
half-sour pickles, three for ten cents. I'd eat more than I'd sell!" she said, laugh-
ing. These were small cucumbers, like large gherkins, but made in the half-sour
fashion, which she describes as cucumbers "well done." There were other
things, like spicy pickled green tomatoes and barrels of sauerkraut. The sours,
her favorite, were larger pickles and sold inside the store from 500-pound
wooden pickle barrels. They also sold borscht (beet soup) from barrels.

Her mother, Jean, had a very good rapport with the customers, especially
the neighborhood women whose sons were in the service. "This would be during World War II," Evelyn continued. "Back then, if a son was in the service,
people would put up stars on pieces of cloth and hang it in their windows at
home. And whenever too much time would go by without hearing any news, a
mother (mostly mothers) would come in and just want to talk."

"In the winter, everything would go indoors so I'd help out inside," said
Evelyn. "When you walked into the store, the counter would be first and then
the barrels were toward the back. Some things were bought prepared and my
mom made some things, like cole slaw and potato salad. My mom made the
best coleslaw! She also made pickled herring and pickled lox."

The store closed in 1957. When asked if she knows how to make any of her
mother's recipes, she responds, "No, my husband is a better cook than I am."
She says he's Irish-English but makes great Italian food.

VIZES UBORKA
(Hungarian Sun Pickles)

MAKES 1 GALLON

25 to 30 small Kirby cucumbers,
up to 5 inches long
1 bunch fresh dill
4 or 5 cloves garlic, peeled and
crushed
4 quarts water
6 tablespoons coarse salt (kosher or
pickling)
1 teaspoon all-purpose flour
1 thick slice rye or sourdough bread
(see Note)

Wash and scrub the cucumbers well. Cut off both ends and carefully make a lengthwise cut down the center of each one, leaving about 1 inch intact on either end so they don't fall apart. This lets the liquid reach the inside of the cucumber.

Place some of the dill and garlic in the bottom of a 1-gallon jar. Tightly pack a layer of cucumbers upright in the jar. Add more of the dill and garlic and another layer of packed cucumbers. Continue to alternate layers, leaving about 1-inch free at the top of the jar.

Place a clean, raised rack in the bottom of a big, nonreactive pot. Put the water and salt in the pot and bring to a boil. Stand the packed pickle jar in the very hot water (on the rack, so it won't crack), and ladle the hot salted water into the jar to cover the cucumbers. Sprinkle the flour on top (do not stir) and press on the slice of bread.

Screw on the lid and place the jar outside in a sunny area, or in a warm place indoors if the weather turns cool. You can bring the jar inside at night, but check every day to be sure the liquid still fills the jar so the bread doesn't dry out. Add warm water if it evaporates somewhat.

After 4 to 5 days of pickling, your sun pickles should be ready to eat. Discard the bread, take out the pickles, and strain the brine through a fine-meshed sieve. Put the pickles back in the jar and pour the strained brine over them. They will keep well for about 1 week if refrigerated. By then you'll want to make another batch.

Note: Be sure to use good-quality bread. Store-bought is okay, but bakery bread is best, because the yeast in it makes the fermentation process work. Theresa likes to use the end piece or heel.

J*erilyn *J. Gates is a professor and chef at the New York Restaurant School. When her mother became ill, she wanted to preserve her mother's legendary pickle recipes for her own daughter and her new grandbaby. These pickles are part of an important family tradition. By interviewing her mother about pickle-making and recording her pickle recipes, Jerri was able to capture a taste of her childhood to share with family and friends.

"On my mother's ninety-first birthday. I was able to enjoy a quiet moment listening to her talk about her early childhood. She was the sixth child in a family of fourteen children. Work was her only form of play. The large family of eight boys and six girls demanded constant food preparation and cook-fire maintenance. Prepping vegetables and firewood were two of mother's tasks. She fondly remembers the large pots of potatoes she and her mother prepared, the smell of bread baking in the wood stove, and the vision of her father coming home from his work as a logging-camp cook with baskets that were fashioned from strips of birch bark and fastened with his leather shoelaces. If he had wild berries, everyone knew it was shortcake for supper.

"When my now-adult daughter was younger, my mother taught her and her friend to make crock pickles. Both of the little girls went home with a quart of homemade pickles. They were so proud of their accomplishment, and the tradition was passed to another generation.

"These recipes are from my mother. The pickles are strongly flavored and to most an acquired taste. While she shared other recipes with me, it was apparent that the crock pickle recipe is her favorite from nearly a century ago."

These pickles are very similar to the mustard pickles my own grandmother kept in the refrigerator (see page 31). The brine contains no water, so the taste is strong and undiluted, which I enjoy very much. They are mustard-hot but won't blow you away.

(continued on next page)

GRAM'S CROCK PICKLES

MAKES 3 QUARTS

**3 pounds Kirby cucumbers, small
or large, scrubbed**
4 cups cider vinegar
**¼ cup coarse salt (kosher or
pickling)**
¼ cup sugar
¼ cup powdered mustard

Cut ¼ inch from the stem end of
each cucumber, then rub the cut
ends together vigorously to remove
any bitterness. Discard the end
pieces, cut the cucumbers in spears,
and seeds them. Tightly pack the
cucumber spears in quart-sized jars
or a ceramic pickling crock.

In a large, nonreactive bowl mix
together the vinegar, salt, sugar,
and powdered mustard. Pour the
brine over the cucumbers to cover,
then screw the lids on the jars or
cover the crock.

Let the pickles rest undisturbed
for at least 2 days, or until the
bright green cucumbers turn light
brown in color. They are ready
to eat.

Store the jars in the refrigerator, or the crock, if using, in a root
cellar or other cool, dark place.
Keptcool, these pickles will stay
crisp for about 1 month, but will
remain edible for about 6 months.

Jerri has recipes from her mother and her aunt, so there's quite a family pickle legacy to pass down through the generations. Thanksgiving just isn't the same without Tongue Pickles and Elephant Ears (see page 44) on the table—both are family favorites.

The name rises from a simple matter of opinion. After the cucumbers have been pickled they turn a brownish color, and because of the way the pickles have been sliced, Jerri swears that they look just like tongues.

TONGUE PICKLES

MAKES 4 PINTS

6 to 7 large cucumbers, about 5½
  pounds, peeled, cut in half first
  lengthwise then widthwise, then
  seeded
2 pounds dark brown sugar
1 tablespoon coarse salt (kosher
  or pickling)
2 cups cider vinegar
1 tablespoon whole cloves
1 tablespoon ground ginger
1 tablespoon ground cinnamon,
  or 2 cinnamon sticks
½ tablespoon black peppercorns

Place the cucumber pieces in a large, nonreactive pot. Add the brown sugar, salt, and vinegar, then tie the cloves, ginger, cinnamon, and peppercorns in a cheesecloth and add it to pot. Bring to a boil over medium heat, and continue to cook until the cucumbers are transparent and the liquid has turned to syrup, about 45 minutes. Pour the cucumbers with the syrup into a large bowl, cover, and refrigerate for 12 hours or overnight.

The next morning, reheat and transfer to sterilized pint-sized jars (see pages 12–14). Allow ½ inch head space, but make sure the syrup completely covers the cucmbers. Screw on the lids and process in a hot-water bath for 10 minutes to seal. Allow to cool completely before sealing. Eat immediately or store in the cupboard for up to 12 months. Refrigerate after opening.

Note: This recipe can also be made using late-season green tomatoes instead of cucumbers.

In a fashion typical of passed down recipes, Jerri Gates gave me this recipe with measurements that were based on her grandmother's coffee mugs. These sweet pickles are made with large, late-season cucumbers, which have large tough seeds and a bitter peel, and make good use of cucumbers you otherwise might be inclined to toss. And, yes, they do resemble long elephant ears (but should not be mistaken for the funnel cakes sold by the same name at Midwestern U.S. county fairs).

ELEPHANT EARS

MAKES 4 QUARTS

3 quarts water
1 cup coarse salt (kosher or pickling)
10 to 11 large cucumbers, 7 pounds, peeled, cut in half lengthwise, and seeded
3 coffee mugs (4½ cups) distilled white vinegar
5 coffee mugs (7½ cups) water
2 coffee mugs (3 cups) sugar
2 pounds dark brown sugar
3 teaspoons ground cinnamon, or 2 cinnamon sticks
2 teaspoons whole cloves

In a large, nonreactive bowl or pickling crock, mix together the water and salt, add the cucumbers, and soak for 12 hours or overnight. Take the cucumbers out of the water, drain in a colander, and set aside.

In a large, nonreactive pot, combine the vinegar, water, sugar, brown sugar, cinnamon, and cloves. Bring to a boil, mixing regularly with a wooden spoon. Once a thin syrup has formed, about 5 minutes, add the cucumber halves and return to a boil. Lower the heat and simmer until the cucumbers are tender and the liquid has reduced to a thin syrup once again, about 20 minutes.

Sterilize the quart-sized jars and lids according to the directions on pages 12–14. Pour the mixture into the jars, screw on the lids, and process in a hot-water bath for 10 minutes to seal. Let cool. Enjoy immediately or store in a cupboard for up to 1 year. Refrigerate after opening.

Another of Jerri's family recipes is also good for using up late season cucumbers. Although the ingredients are similar to those for Elephant Ears, the flavor of these pickles is distinctly different.

SWEET CUKE PICKLES

1 tablespoon coarse salt (kosher or pickling)
1½ tablespoons dark brown sugar
2 cups distilled white vinegar
5 to 6 large cucumbers, 5 pounds, peeled, cut in half lengthwise, seeded, and then into large chunks

For the Spice Bag
1 tablespoon ground cloves
1 tablespoon ground ginger
1 tablespoon ground cinnamon
½ tablespoon black pepper

In a large, nonreactive pot, combine the salt, brown sugar, vinegar, and spice bag (you can simply put the spices in a piece of cheesecloth and tie it with cotton kitchen twine). Add the chunks of cucumber and bring to a boil over high heat. Reduce the heat and simmer until the cucumbers are tender, 1 to 2 hours. Allow the mixture to cool, then pour it into a large nonreactive bowl, cover, and refrigerate for 12 hours or overnight.

In the morning, reheat the pickles and brine, then transfer them to sterilized pint-sized jars (see pages 12–14), making sure the brine completely covers the pickles while leaving ¼ inch free at the top of the jars. Screw on the lids and process in a hot-water bath for 10 minutes to seal. Eat immediately or store in the cupboard for up to 12 months. Refrigerate after opening.

The Legacy of Guss' Pickles

There is so much pickling history in Manhattan's Lower East Side, and in many ways the stories run parallel to each other. Despite the many obstacles of making a business thrive in New York City, Tim Baker, of Guss' Pickles, keeps the company afloat. In the fall of 2001, Guss' moved into a storefront in the Lower East Side Tenement Museum building on Orchard Street, just blocks from the store's historic long-time Essex Street site. Recently the business moved to a private space downtown on Orchard Street.

"In 1979 my father bought Guss' Pickles with his partner, Burt Blitz, who owned Hollander Pickles, otherwise known as L. Hollander and Sons. (Burt was the son-in-law of Natie Hollander.) Izzy Guss was the original owner of Guss' Pickles. Izzy got here in about 1910 and originally worked for Louis Hollander, who was Natie's father. He worked for a week and didn't get paid. So he said, 'I'll teach him!' and he went and started his own pushcart. He bought a couple bushels of cucumbers and he started pickling stuff himself. When Guss ran his pushcart, he and Hollander were in friendly competition one block away from each other.

"Before Hunts Point [the world's largest food distribution center, where all the produce for the millions of New Yorkers enters the city everyday], there were sections of the city where you could find different kinds of produce. It wasn't centralized in one spot. The cucumbers were on Ludlow Street. That's why there were so many pickle stores there. There were over a hundred pickle stores in that neighborhood fifty years ago. When I started twenty-two years ago, there were only four stores. And now there's only one original store left, and we are having a hard time making it.

"Saul Kaplan was one of the people who taught me the business. He had a store called Kaplan Pickles on Orchard near Rivington. In 1969 he was on his way home from synagogue and he was stabbed while being robbed. His family wanted him to close the store, so he closed it and went to go work for his friend, Izzy Guss. When Izzy passed away, Saul stayed with Izzy's brother, Benny Guss. Benny just passed away about two years ago. The only one living now is Natie. Kaplan died about four years ago. He was nineteen years old when he bought his own pickle store.

"You know, in Russia, their families were also in the pickle business, so this is the only thing that they knew. Benny Guss, the first day he came here from Russia, he walked from downtown Battery Park all the way up to Harlem because he had no place to stay. He didn't know where he was going to go or what he was going to do. Downtown everyone spoke Yiddish. There were like two hundred to three hundred thousand Jews. So that's why they went there. It was the only way for them to communicate. I think that had a lot to do with why they wanted to go into the pickle business—that's what they knew.

"Rabbis supervise all the ingredients that go into our pickles. They make sure that everything is kosher and that the barrels are not used for anything else. The store is also closed during the Sabbath. We close on Fridays and all Jewish holidays. Without Passover, I'd be out of business. We grind fresh horse-radish, we're the only place in the city. During Passover, there's always a two-hour line. Two weeks before Passover, the line begins to stretch up to the corner. I could go home at one o'clock and I'm back at five o'clock and there are people in line in front of the store before I get there. It's the same thirty people in line who have stood in line for Passover for the last thirty years, maybe more.

"It's more important that I keep Guss' going for the old men because they thought the only way this thing would keep going is if I made sure it did. I managed it for ten years and they were talking of closing because it was basically going out of business. So I assumed all the debt and took over the store. The old men were behind me and helped me out financially.

"There's a need for the store to be there. It's a piece of history, but more than that, it's a part of people's lives. Just last Sunday I was working at the store and this young guy came in with a three year old on his back. My grandmother brought me here, too. You know, I find a little tiny pickle and I give it to the kid, and the kid drops the pacifier on the ground, grabs the pickle, and starts eating it. This is job security for me. This kid is going to learn what a good pickle tastes like: He'll know the difference. The reason why this couple drove from Jersey to walk around the Lower East Side was to show their kids what their grandmother and grandfather brought them to see years before. That's what's important."

Despite Guss' financial hardship in recent years, Andrew Leibowitz, eldest son of Steve Leibowitz of United Pickle Products (see page 53) announced in 2002 the creation of Crossing Delancy Pickle Enterprise Corp. As it happens, Tim joined forces with Andrew in order to save the legendary Lower East Side business. As a pleasant surpise to many New Yorkers, Andrew announced plans for future expansion by opening Guss' Pickles retail store in Cedarhurst, New York. As president of the new company, Andrew, along with Tim, envisions future expansion for Guss'. Meanwhile, Tim Baker spends his time at the Manhattan location. If Andrew and Tim have their way, Americans will go back to buying kosher pickles straight from the barrels—just like they used to.

This recipe for fresh pickles from Yelena and Vladimir Groysman is easy and helps you avoid the excesses of the store-bought kind—these pickles won't be too sour or too salty. Vladimir says this about the origin of the recipe: "I lived in Latvostok, near China, in Russia. This place, it was a hard time in wintertime. Not like here where you go to the store and you buy pickles. We prepared food for wintertime. Now we don't need this. We go to the stores, but sometimes, the food just doesn't have the right taste—or *vkus*. When we have a guest, we put my pickles on the table. It's more special. People like this. I almost forgot something that makes this recipe delicious—black currant leaves. Before your guests come, you fix this pickle at least two days before."

Although the recipe that follows is directly as it came from Vladimir, I like these pickles with a full tablespoon of salt and left mine in the refrigerator for 3 weeks before eating them. You can substitute cherry leaves for the black currant leaves—or you can make the recipe without any leaves at all.

GROYSMAN'S FRESH PICKLES WITH BLACK CURRANT LEAVES

MAKES 2 QUARTS

30 to 35 small Kirby cucumbers, each about 3 inches long
1 to 2 sprigs fresh dill
6 black peppercorns
4 cloves garlic, peeled and split
2 teaspoons coarse salt (kosher or pickling)
1 small piece (about 1 inch) fresh horseradish, peeled and halved
1 to 2 black currant leaves

Scrub the cucumbers then score the top and bottom of each with a 1-inch-deep X. Pack them tightly into a 2-quart jar, then where ever you can find room, add the dill, pepper- corns, garlic, salt, horseradish, and black currant leaves. Fill the jar almost to the top with cold boiled water and screw on the lid.

Store in a cool, dark place and you will have good half-sours in 3 days, or wait a few days longer for your desired acidity. To stop the pickles from getting too sour, simply refrigerate them. If you are reluc- tant to use this pickling method, store the pickles in the refrigerator immediately and allow the flavors to develop for 3 weeks before tasting. Refrigerated, these will keep for about 1 month, but you will have eaten them all long before then.

*F*or twenty-six years, **Sophia Vinokurau** has run M & I International Foods in Brighton Beach, Brooklyn, with her brother, sister, and husband. She is originally from Odessa, Russia, and came to the United States only two years before opening the store. There they make and sell pickles based on recipes from back home. Including a salty-sweet pickle made from watermelon slices tangled in fresh dill (page 127) and golden apples pickled with cabbage and salt to be served cold alongside meat (page 128). And year round, they sell these delicious bright green cucumber pickles brined with water and salt with a touch of vodka rather than vinegar.

Says Sophia, "Watermelon pickles. Cucumber pickles. Soft cabbage pickles. Tomato pickles. The Russians, they eat a lot of pickles! In Russia you used to prepare things for the whole year. My mother used to make these pickles, and I remember there was a special cabinet where she held them all."

There is very little vodka in this recipe so if the alcohol concerns you feel free to omit it. After a few weeks in the refrigerator the pickles become sort of "fizzy"; this is when you know they are at their best!

PICKLED KIRBY WITH VODKA

MAKES 3 PINTS

1 tablespoon plus 1 teaspoon
  coarse salt (kosher or pickling)
1 teaspoon pickling spice
2 teaspoons vodka
½ teaspoon hot red pepper flakes
3½ cups cold water
3 cloves garlic, peeled and
  crushed
¼ cup diced celery
8 medium-sized Kirby cucumbers,
  about 1 pound, whole, halved, or
  quartered
2 tablespoons fresh dill

In a large, nonreactive bowl or pot, mix the salt, pickling spice, vodka, and red pepper flakes with the cold water to create a brine. Set aside.

Sterilize the jars and lids according to the directions on pages 12–14. Put equal portions of the garlic and celery in the bottom of each pint-sized jar. Next pack in the cucumbers, adding a generous portion of dill to each jar, stem sides down. Pour in the brine until it reaches about 1 inch from the lip of each jar. Tightly screw on the lids and refrigerate for 2 to 3 weeks.

Note: While the pickles are edible after 2 weeks, they reach their peak flavor at 3 to 4 weeks. After a month of storage, they become soggy and sour.

***S**ol Weinberg was rasied* on a "pickle farm" near Albany in Stephentown, New York. In addition to cucumbers, the family grew sweet corn. In fact, they grew a lot of it, up to 200 acres, which they sold at the Bronx Terminal Market. The whole family took part in tending the 3 to 4 acres of cucumber vines. Back then, they raised Boston pickling cucumbers, a variety of Kirby.

In the 1930s, the family pickled about one hundred and fifty 55-gallon barrels of cucumbers and pickled them in salt, water, dill, or pickling spice, according to the recipe given to them by Cohen Pickles in Staten Island. Several times a month, after Sol turned sixteen, he would drive the family's 1936 Dodge truck—loaded with wooden barrels full of briny pickles—as far as Yonkers, north of New York City. There a train would transport them the rest of the way to Cohen's. They were paid one dollar per bushel of cucumbers.

Sol eventually left the family farm for Manhattan, where he worked in the more lucrative business of selling insurance. One of his clients was Omanoff Pickles on Stebbins Avenue in the Bronx. Sol remembers his fondness for the family and especially Max Omanoff, a terrific salesman who also made the best-tasting, partially ripe pink tomato pickles he has ever eaten.

Even though Sol hasn't worked on the farm in years, he still remembers his time there as the good old days. "It was very hard work, but I loved it!" he explains. Sol's brother Si Weinberg has a family recipe for fresh dill pickles that are so crisp, delicious, and easy to prepare. They are green, fresh tasting, and worth waiting for—it takes three weeks until they ferment to perfection.

SI WEINBERG'S DILL PICKLES

MAKES 2 QUARTS

10 to 12 firm green Kirby
  cucumbers, no larger than
  4 inches long and 1½-inches wide
4 sprigs fresh dill, long stems
  removed
4 cloves garlic, peeled and coarsely
  chopped
¼ cup coarse salt (kosher or
  pickling)
¼ cup pickling spice

Scrub the cucumbers under cold running water, then drain them in a colander.

Sterilize the jars and lids according to the directions on pages 12–14. Place two sprigs dill, stems side down, in each quart-sized jar. Then tightly pack the cucumbers in the jars, starting with the largest cucumber and ending with the smallest. Sprinkle half the garlic into each jar, then add equal portions of the salt and pickling spice.

Fill the jars with enough cold water to cover the cucumbers. Place the caps on the jars and tightly screw on the lids. Shake the contents until the salt dissolves and the garlic and pickling spice are distributed evenly throughout. Store in a cool, dark place (like a root cellar) or in the back of a refrigerator. The pickles will be ready to taste in 3 to 4 weeks.

Once you are satisfied with the sourness of the pickles, remove them and set aside in a nonreactive bowl. Pour the brine through a fine-mesh strainer, discarding the solids (garlic, pickling spice, and dill).

Repack the pickles in the same jars and pour in the strained brine. Add enough cold water to cover the pickles. Refrigerated, they will stay fresh for 1 month or longer.

Variation: To make these pickles spicy, add ¼ cup hot red pepper flakes along with the pickling spice.

Theresa Rose is an actor who lives in New York. She and her siblings were each given a recipe book filled with family favorites, including these 24-hour pickles. They are easy to make and mild enough to suit all tastes.

24-HOUR PICKLES

MAKES 4 PINTS

6 cups English cucumbers, about
    6 cucumbers, scrubbed and thinly
    sliced
2 cups thinly sliced cups onion (for
    bite-sized pickles, use only the
    small, inner rings)
1½ cups sugar
1½ cups distilled white vinegar
½ teaspoon coarse salt (kosher or
    pickling)
½ teaspoon white mustard seed
½ teaspoon celery seed
½ teaspoon turmeric

Alternately layer cucumber then onion slices in a large, nonreactive bowl; set aside.

Combine the remaining ingredients in a small saucepan and bring to a boil over medium-high heat. Pour the hot brine over the cucumbers and onions, and leet them soak for about 5 minutes.

Sterilize the jars and lids according to the directions on pages 12–14. Divide the vegetables and brine among the pint-sized jars and tightly screw on the lids. Refrigerate for at least 24 hours and up to 2 months before eating.

Harry "Teddy" Weishaus first set foot in Manhattan in 1913 when he began working with his uncle, an already established Lower East Side pickle-maker who had paid for his twenty-five-dollar passage from Ternopol, Poland. Some years later, Teddy took over the company and taught one of his sons, Ury, the trade. Ury then passed the pickle, so to speak, to his son Marvin.

Then there was the Leibowitz family. Max left his wife and children in Molochansk, Russia, in 1925 to set sail for what he believed to be the golden land of opportunity. He found employment in a grocery store, where he paid close attention to its pickle sales. Soon he opened one of New York's first pickle stands at what would become a legendary address for pickles, 35 Essex Street. After just one year, he had saved enough to bring his family to America. His two sons, David and Leon, created a wholesale-pickle empire, which was passed down to David's son, Steve.

In 1979 these two legendary pickle families joined forces, creating the United Pickle Company. Together partners Steve Leibowitz and Marvin Weishaus, both third-generation pickle men, developed the largest Jewish-owned pickle company in the country. United is housed in the Bronx in the former Borden Dairy. There it produces more than 70 million pickles each year, including products for as many as twenty brands from coast to coast. United makes some of the best-tasting, most authentic New York sours and half-sours, which are sold at New York landmarks like Nathan's and the Carnegie Deli. United also sells and ships pickle spears and pickle chips, pickled tomatoes, sweet and hot peppers, sweet and dill relishes, and sauerkraut.

One year Steve and his wife were invited to visit with a group of Jewish senior citizens in Brooklyn. The seniors told them many personal stories and shared memories of when his father and grandfather ran their pickle stands. It was then that Steve realized what his family legacy meant to people's lives. The word got out about the success of his visit to the senior center, and soon he and a group of local business and political leaders came up with an idea to celebrate pickles in a way that would reflect the pickle's role as a New York icon. In 1994 United cosponsored its first pickle-eating contest, now held at the Second Avenue Deli and Carnegie Deli every two years.

(continued on next page)

Steve Leibowitz, his wife, and their two sons celebrated the First Annual NY International Pickle Day with the NY Food Museum on September 30, 2001. It was an extremely chilly and wet day for that time of year, yet people came out in droves. Together, Steve and his family sold pickles from under a tent on Orchard Street, just blocks from his grandfather's original storefront. Steve and his wife also celebrated their wedding anniversary that day, meeting pickle fans fact-to-face as they rarely did while selling to wholesalers. It was a day worth celebrating!

This recipe for sour pickles was developed by operations manager Jose Torres, Jr., (the son of the former boxing champion) and co-owner Marvin Weishaus. It tastes similar to United's famous, but well-guarded, secret recipe. Don't be shocked by the addition of Tums tablets in this recipe; they not only keep the pickles crunchy, but add calcium as well.

HOME-CURED SOUR PICKLES

MAKES 1 GALLON

2 cups distilled white vinegar
¾ cups coarse salt (kosher or pickling)
2 nonflavored Tums tablets, crushed
18 to 22 medium-sized Kirby cucumbers, about 4½ pounds
1½ teaspoons pickling spice
1 to 2 tablespoons chopped garlic cloves
1 to 2 sprigs fresh dill

In a 1-gallon jar, combine the vinegar, salt, and Tums tablets. Fill the jar with lukewarm water and stir until the salt and Tums have dissolved to create a brine.

In another 1-gallon jar, begin to pack the cucumbers as tightly as possible without bruising them. Halfway through packing the jar, add the pickling spice, garlic, and dill, stem side down, then finish packing the cucumbers.

Slowly pour the brine into the pickle jar until the cucumbers are completely covered; reserve the excess brine in a covered container (see Note). Cap the jar and shake it, turning it upside down a few times to break up any air pockets that may have developed.

To ferment the pickles, loosen the cap so that carbon dioxide can escape. Place the jar on a large plate to catch any spills, as the brine may foam and overflow. Store the jar in a moderately warm place (80° to 85°F) for 5 to 9 days, until the cucumbers change from bright green to a light brownish-green, especially around the stem ends.

Once or twice within the fermentation period, tighten the cap and turn the jar upside down four or five times to loosen gas pockets and ensure even curing. If some liquid has evaporated and the pickles are protruding above the surface of the brine, add 1 to 2 tablespoons of the reserved brine and gently flip the jar to mix. Be sure to loosen the cap again after each handling.

When the pickles have changed color completely, place the jar in the refrigerator for 48 hours to stop the fermentation process. They are ready to eat. Store in the refrigerator.

Note: Although a gallon of brine is more than the pickles initially require, you may need some during the curing process. You can always use the rest in future batches: It never goes bad.

***M**ary Snead, the daughter of* a Baptist preacher, moved from Texas to New York City twenty years ago. There she met and married her love, Henry, a Jewish attorney. When Mary's mother sent them her homemade pickles, Henry loved them so much he would make an entire meal out of mounds of pickles stacked on a plate. To make sure that Henry always would have as many pickles as he could eat, Mary set out to learn how to make her mother's pickles. Using only the freshest produce from the Jewish markets on Avenue J in Brooklyn, Mary now makes some of the tastiest homemade pickles around. She ferments them in her basement in her own 3-gallon crock, and occasionally pickles enough to share with her neighbors.

Mary approached me at our first Pickle Day. She had brought along samples for me to taste. Gladly and happily I indulged. Both of Mary's recipes—Mother's Pickles and Winter Dills—prove that homemade pickle are far superior to mass produced.

Alum (see page 17) was once a very common ingredient in pickle recipes. It was used to prevent pickles from becoming soft and soggy. I found my alum powder at my local pharmacist even though the directions on the label clearly state that it is for pickling. Use only the amount called for, and while it can be omitted I don't know of any substitute. It is safe to use but I wouldn't suggest eating it every day.

Since alum's active ingredient is aluminum, please make certain that your cooking equipment is all stainless steel, plastic, wood, or earthenware, all of which are nonreactive materials.

MOTHER'S PICKLES

MAKES 5 PINTS

30 small cucumbers, about 6
   pounds, scrubbed and thinly
   sliced
1 cup plus 1 tablespoon coarse salt
   (kosher or pickling)
3 gallons plus 2 cups water
1 tablespoon alum powder (see
   page 17)
1 tablespoon ground ginger
1 tablespoon celery seed or
   white mustard seed
6 cups sugar
4 cups distilled white vinegar

Put the cucumbers in a 1-gallon pickling crock. Combine the 1 cup of salt and 1 gallon of water in a large, nonreactive bowl, and stir until the salt dissolves. Pour the salted water over the cucumbers, cover the crock with a clean dish towel, and secure it with a string or rubber band. Stir once a day for 6 days, returning the cloth covering each time. At the end of 6 days, drain the cucumbers in a colander, rinse in 1 gallon of the water, and return the cucumbers to the crock.

In a large, nonreactive bowl, combine the third gallon of water with the alum. Pour the solution over the cucumbers, cover with a clean dish towel secured with a string or rubber band, and let soak for 12 hours or overnight. The next morning, drain the cucumbers in a colander and rinse them under cold running water, then return them to the crock.

In a nonreactive pot, combine the ginger, celery seed, sugar, and vinegar, plus the remaining 1 tablespoon salt and 2 cups water, and mix well. Bring to a boil over high heat, then add the cucumbers and return to a boil for about 10 minutes, until the cucumbers are transparent.

In the meantime, sterilize the jars and lids according to the directions on pages 12–14. Fill the pint-sized jars, leaving 1 inch of headspace, and screw on the lids, and process them in a hot-water bath for 10 to 15 minutes. Allow to cool, then store the jars in a cupboard for up to 6 months.

WINTER DILLS

30 small cucumbers, about
  6 pounds
6 tablespoons dill seed
6 sprigs fresh dill
½ teaspoon alum powder (see
  page 17)
½ teaspoon minced garlic
3 teaspoons white mustard seed
3 cups distilled white vinegar
6 tablespoons coarse salt
  (kosher or pickling)
7 cups water

In a 1-gallon crock or jar, cover the cucumbers with cold water and cover the crock with a lid. Soak for 12 hours or overnight. The next morning, scrub the cucumbers with a brush, rinse with more cold water, and drain in a colander.

Sterilize the jars and lids according to the directions on pages 12–14. Pack the cucumbers into the quart-sized jars and add the following to each jar: 1 tablespoon dill seed, 1 sprig dill weed, stems and frond, ⅛ teaspoon alum, ⅛ teaspoon minced garlic, and ½ teaspoon mustard seed.

In a large saucepan, combine the water, vinegar, and salt. Bring to a boil and then pour, boiling hot, over the cucumbers, leaving ¼ inch free at the top of the jars. Screw on the lids and process them in a hot-water bath for 10 minutes to seal.

Allow to cool, then store the jars in a cupboard. Should the pickles ferment (see Note), wait another week before opening them and then pour off the old brine and replace it with a fresh batch of new brine. They will be ready to eat.

Note: Mary uses the word "ferment" to describe the "fizzy" quality a brine can develop because of yeast activation. This is desirable in salt-brined pickles, but not in those that are vinegar brined.

Dean's Pickles

In the heart of Arkansas lies Atkins, a proud little town with a meager population of about 3,000. Back in 1946, the Goldsmith Pickle Company built their manufacturing plant and started producing pickle products there. In 1983 Dean's Food Company purchased Goldsmith's, adding it to a growing subsidiary called Green Bay Foods Company with a home base in Wisconsin. After years of investing in the Atkins plant, Dean's Pickle outpost in Atkins became one of the leading pickled cucumber and pepper packers in the United States.

Atkins' proud residents hold a Pickle Fest every summer (see page 153). They have contests for pickle eating and pickle-juice drinking, and a pickle pageant where girls and boys are awarded grand titles (Baby Sweet Pickles and Baby Dill Pickles; Little Miss Sweet Pickles and Mr. Dill Pickles). There is usually a horseshoe toss, adventure sight-seeing "pickle" train rides for kids, a 5K race, local music performances, arts and crafts, and even a rodeo.

Fried dill pickles are one of many "chicken-fried" favorites originating in the South. They are often associated with Elvis Presley, whose favorite fried foods led to his weight gain, but he did not invent the recipe. That honor goes to none other than Atkins' own Bernell "Fat Man" Austin, who claims to have invented the recipe for the fried dill pickle. In fact, Bernell's wife Sue attends Pickle Fests to sell this unusual treat to Fest guests. No one seems to doubt its true origin.

Among the many casualties of the recession in 2002, Dean's Pickles permanently closed its doors in June, after fifty years as the largest industry in Atkins. The closing obviously put a strain on local employment figures and took its toll on city revenues as well. The parent company in Green Bay still maintains the Dean's Pickles and Specialty Foods brands in several other areas of the country.

To mark the last day of the stock line at the pickle plant, a local baker named Wayne Cheek designed and presented a cake to the plant's employees. A card placed to the side of the cake read, "Wishing each of you a 'sweet' ending to a 'sour' deal!"

*T*his is my grandmother's recipe," says Mary Katherine Moore. "The original recipe was from my great-grandmother's friend Gladys of Holly Springs, Mississippi. We all loved these pickles served with bland things like peas and cornbread. They are syrup-brown, have a very sweet-tart flavor, and are quite crisp. I was also intrigued by the fact that they were shaped like long squared off sticks and had no seeds, which I hated as a child. This pickle makes great use of cucumbers that have been left on the vine too long. The large ones have more flesh to make into the long sticks."

Mary Katherine entered these pickles into the 2002 Alabama State Fair competition and won third place. Her prize was a check for one dollar. Nonetheless, Mary Katherine says, "I'm very happy with the third place win, as the competition was stiff!"

GLAD'S PICKLES

MAKES 1 DOZEN PINTS

2 cups lime (see page 20)
12 pounds large ripe cucumbers, peeled, seeded, and cut into square sticks (yields 7 pounds)
¼ cup alum powder (see page 17)
10 cups white vinegar
14 cups sugar
1 teaspoon coarse salt (kosher or pickling)
1 tablespoon celery seed
3 tablespoons pickling spice

Make a solution of the lime and 1 gallon water, or enough to cover the cucumber sticks in an earthenware crock. Let them soak for 48 hours or 2 days. Rinse under cold running water and drain in a colander. Return the cucumbers to the crock. Make a new solution from the alum and 1 gallon water and pour over the pickles to cover.

Cover with a plate or lid and let stand for 6 hours. Rinse again with water and drain. Let soak in another gallon of water for 5 or 6 hours, then rinse and drain in a colander.

Put the cucumbers in a large, nonreactive pot. Combine 2½ quarts water, the vinegar, sugar, salt, celery seed, and the pickling spice, pour the mixture over the cucumbers, and bring to a boil. Remove from heat, allow to cool, and let sit until morning, about 12 hours. Return the pot to a boil and cook until the cucumbers are transparent, about 1 hour.

In the meantime, sterilize the jars and lids according to the directions on pages 12–14. Fill the pint-sized jars, screw on the lids, and process in a hot-water bath for 10 minutes to seal. Allow the jars to cool and store in cupboard for up to 1 year.

This particular recipe has been in Françoise Raimbault's family for more than four generations. She was born and still lives in Tours, in the heart of the Loire Valley in France.

Françoise really enjoys making this recipe because they are far superior to store-bought pickles. Her family also loves them, which is how the recipe became a part of this collection. Françoise's daughter, Sophie, a professional hairstylist in Manhattan, says her mother has always made them from scratch and never follows an exact recipe. When I asked her if she personally liked her mother's recipe, she replied in earnest, "Trust me, they are very good!"

CORNICHONS

MAKES 1 LITER (A LITTLE MORE
THAN 1 QUART)

2½ pounds gherkin cucumbers
   (tiny dark-green cucumbers
   grown especially for pickling)
2 cups distilled white vinegar
1 cup non-iodized sea salt
6 garlic cloves, peeled and left
   whole
2 tablespoon white peppercorns
1 sprig fresh tarragon or dill
   (optional)
7 fresh pearl onions, peeled and
   left whole

Sterilize a 1 quart jar and lid according to the directions on pages 12–14. Wash the gherkins by rubbing them against each other under cold running water. Drain them in a colander, then dry with a clean dish towel. Transfer the gherkins to a large, nonreactive bowl, add the salt, and let them marinate for about 4 hours. Stir with a spoon every once in a while to distribute the salt and the liquid that will develop. Rinse the gherkins again under cold running water, drain and dry them, using another clean towel, being careful not to break or bruise them.

Tightly pack the gherkins in the still-hot jar, along with the garlic, peppercorn, tarragon, and pearl onions; leave as little space as possible. Bring the vinegar to a boil in a saucepan and pour it carefully over the vegetables, leaving about 1 inch free at the top of the jar. Screw on the lid and process the jar in a hot-water bath for 10 minutes to seal (see pages 12–14). The jar must be stored in a cool, dry place for at least 2 to 3 months before using. Unopened, they can be kept for up to 2 years. Refrigerate after opening.

The history of deep-fried dill pickles may be traced back to Atkins, Arkansas, the home of the Atkins Pickle Fest and the "inventor" of this crispy pickle, Bernell "Fat Man" Austin. Recipe ingredients differ widely, but for the best flavor and texture, I prefer mine made with a buttermilk and white cornmeal batter similar to my favorite fried-green tomato batter. I think Elvis would be proud.

DEEP-FRIED DILL PICKLES

MAKES 4 TO 6 SMALL SERVINGS

1 quart dill pickles, either spears or chips
2 large eggs
2¼ cups all-purpose flour
1 cup buttermilk
½ teaspoon vinegar-based hot sauce, such as Tabasco Sauce
⅛ teaspoon cayenne pepper
1 cup white cornmeal
1 teaspoon salt, plus more to taste
½ teaspoon black pepper, plus more to taste
2 cups vegetable oil

Drain the pickles in a colander. In a mixing bowl, combine the eggs, ¼ cup of the flour, buttermilk, hot sauce, and cayenne pepper. In a second mixing bowl, combine the cornmeal, the remaining 2 cups flour, and the salt and pepper.

Preheat the oil in a deep fryer or large cast-iron pan until it's hot, about 365°F. Dip the pickles in the buttermilk mixture, dredge them in the flour mixture, then drop them one by one in the pan. Fry until golden brown, about 4 minutes. Drain the fried pickles on paper towels and add more salt and pepper to taste. Serve immediately as an appetizer or snack.

"*Grandma always served pickles,*" Jane Maharam remembers. "Sometimes they came in a barrel from a grocery store and sometimes from a jar. Some sweet; some sour. Great-grandma Jane came from England. She said that the English often served sweet pickles to accompany meals, and since there was a lack of refrigeration, they used preserved condiments.

"My brother Elliot and I were poor eaters. In order to entice us to eat, Grandma used to include pickles on our sandwiches. Elliot's favorite was cream cheese and sweet pickles. I chose American cheese and sour pickle slices. We loved those sandwiches, and as we got older, we fed them to our children, who eat pickles and cheese sandwiches, too."

ELLIOT'S SWEET PICKLE AND CREAM CHEESE SANDWICH

MAKES 1 SANDWICH

Cream cheese
1 sweet pickle
2 slices white sandwich bread

Spread the cream cheese to the desired thickness on one slice of the bread. Thinly slice the sweet pickles and layer the slices on top of the cream cheese. Cover with another slice of bread and cut the sandwich in quarters. Enjoy!

JANE'S AMERICAN CHEESE AND SOURS SANDWICH

MAKES 1 SANDWICH

Bialy roll, sliced in half
Butter
2 slices American cheese
1 sour pickle

Slice the bialy in half and butter both sides. Lay one slice of American cheese and one half of the bialy. Thinly slice the sour pickle and layer the slices on the cheese. Top with the second cheese slice, cover with the other bialy half, and eat

CHAPTER TWO

Cabbage and Other Leafy Greens

CABBAGES ARE ONE OF THE OLDEST VEGETABLES IN THE BRASSICA genus, which also includes broccoli, cauliflower, and kale. They were brought to North America from Germany and the Low Countries in the mid-sixteenth century because settlers were determined to continue their sauerkraut-making traditions.

In this chapter, you will find recipes for the common globe-shaped cabbage (also known as European white cabbage), Brussels sprouts, and Chinese cabbages—including napa and bok choy. I have also discussed leafy greens, such as two recipes for pickled grape leaves brought from Armenia.

Unlike the strong-tasting waxy leaves on round heads of cabbage, Chinese cabbages have thin, crisp, mild leaves. Stir-frying thin strips of Chinese cabbage in hot oil partially reduces the sulphurous smell often associated with cooked cabbage.

The pickle-making stories in this chapter are some of my favorites. I hope you will find them as beautiful and meaningful as I do.

On the previous spread: From left, back to front, Full Moon Cabbage with Pomegranate Juice (page 78), Madeleine Dikranian's Traditional Pickled Grape Leaves (page 80), and Hakusai-Zuke (page 71) amid pomegranates, grape leaves, and a selection of cabbages.

𝒜*nnie Hauk Lawson* is a culinary historian and curator of the Smithsonian Foodways Festival 2001, which celebrated New York foods. Recently she got together with her mother, Jane, to discuss the importance of pickles and pickle-making in Poland. Her nine-year-old daughter, Alana, contributed her insights on the craft of making sauerkraut at home with her mom.

Jane Hauck was born in Mirlitz, near Krakow, Poland, in April 1923. She was raised on a farm, where Jane and her family made *kiscony ogoruki* (pickles soured in brine) throughout the summer as different produce became bountiful. As kids she and her sisters ate cucumbers straight off the vine, but what they loved best was pulling the lid off the pickle barrel to eat the soured pickles.

The pickle crocks, Jane remembers, were 5- to 6-gallon wooden barrels. Whole cucumbers would be cut off the vine at the tail, washed, and then layered with salt; whole dill stems and seeds, and maybe garlic, would be added. Water was then poured over the cucumbers, which were weighed down so they remained submerged. One week produced wonderful fresh-tasting half-sours— exclusively a summer treat. They never had pickles for the winter, because between her mother and father, uncle, aunt, grandparents, and two sisters, they would be eaten almost immediately! Sometimes they drank the cool brine for refreshment. The pigs were fed the leftover dill and other pickling residue in their fodder.

If Jane's family didn't have cucumber pickles to eat in the winter, there was surely *kapusta,* or sauerkraut. The cabbages used to make it were huge: 10 to 15 inches in diameter and up to 15 pounds each. The stems and outer leaves were cut off and given to the cows and pigs. The rest of the cabbage was rinsed, cut into manageable quarters, and then shredded into the barrels with layers of salt in between.

As Alana has learned from conversations with her grandmother, sauerkraut was made in extra-large wooden barrels, usually about 5 feet tall and 3 feet wide, although some were larger. Alana explains "It was the woman's job to shred and salt, but depending on the village's *kapusta* tradition, either the husband or the children were responsible for stomping around in the salted cabbage (with cleaned feet, of course!) to pack it tightly. Sometimes they even played a game

(continued on next page)

of tag in the barrel." After a few weeks, the fermenting cabbage would really start to smell, but then it would neutralize. When it was ready to eat, the sauerkraut was heated and served as a side dish with *kielbasa* (Polish sausage) and potatoes or stuffed into pirogi. As the kraut was used, the brine in the barrels rose. This brine was used to pickle whole cabbages and apples.

After the family moved to Brooklyn in 1938, Jane's father brought fresh vegetables from a pushcart on Havemeyer Street in Greenpoint, and they made pickles in a stone crock left outside on their balcony.

BABCI AND ALANA'S KAPUSTA
(Polish Sauerkraut)

MAKES 1 QUART

2½ pounds green cabbage, about 1 large cabbage, washed, dried, cored and shredded
½ cup coarse salt (kosher or pickling)

Put a 1- to- 2-inch layer of the shredded cabbage in a large, nonreactive bowl. Sprinkle a handful of the salt over the cabbage. Continue layering the cabbage and the salt until you've used it all. Cover with a clean dish towel, add a wooden disk or plate that can fit inside the bowl, and top with a heavy weight (like a brick or a large can of beans).

Refrigerate the bowl or put it in a cool, dark place like a cellar. Every day or two, skim off any foam from the top of the fermenting cabbage and replace the old towel with a clean, dry one. During summer, you may need to add a solution of 1 tablespoon salt dissolved in 1 cup water to keep the cabbage from dehydrating.

The cabbage will become sauerkraut in 1 to 2 weeks. When the sauerkraut is ready, sterilize a 1-quart jar and lid according to the directions on pages 12–14, transfer the sauerkraut, and screw on the lid. Refrigerated and tightly sealed this will keep for 2 to 3 months.

A Crock of Memory

Like many busy twenty-seven-year-old girls, Michelle Gilbert had never thought too much about family recipes, although in a casual conversation, she had once revealed to me that her family heritage was Polish and Jewish. We were both taking the same half-semester course in food preservation at New York University, and our instructor had approved students to work with me on my pickle research for their final research projects. Michelle interviewed her parents about family memories and pickle recipes, expecting nothing. Surprisingly, she returned to class weeks later bearing her grandfather's 5-gallon pickle crock to share her discovery that not only one but both sides of her family had strong pickling traditions.

"My maternal grandparents are originally from Poland and immigrated to Israel, taking with them many traditional Jewish recipes. My mother and aunt remember my grandmother preparing pickles in big glass jars on the back porch. With the high temperatures, the pickles were ready in just a few days. The sisters would eat a whole jar between them, and can still remember the smells of garlic and dill that filled the room.

"When I was young, visiting my paternal grandparents in New Jersey was always fun. They had a beautiful tomato patch on the narrow strip of land between the driveway and the woods that lay at the end of the street. I can still remember going into the garden, filled with big red tomatoes. I would select my favorite ones fresh off the vines and hand them to my grandmother while she gently placed them in her apron. There were cucumbers in the garden but mostly tomatoes. They had so many tomatoes, there were too many to eat and more than they could ever give away.

"My grandfather used to pickle the tomatoes together with some of the cucumbers, which were never as plentiful. Vinegar, salt, water, and pickling spice were poured over the cleaned tomatoes and cucumbers in a 5-gallon salt-glazed stoneware jar, which is well over a century old by now. The jar was covered with cheesecloth and a plate and weighted down by a rock. Then the jar was placed in the northeast corner of the basement, a few feet from the boiler, for several weeks. Unfortunately my grandfather has passed away, and so has his pickle recipe. However, the memories will never pass and the stoneware jar remains in the family."

This recipe comes from Steve Kennedy, a former student at the French Culinary Institute in New York City. He explains, "Many years ago, my mother was exchanging recipes with her neighbor, Lorraine Terry. When my mother asked if she had a recipe for pickled Brussels sprouts, Lorraine volunteered her husband's help. A salesman for Agway farm supplies, he asked the question of all the farm wives on his route and this is the result. We renamed the recipe in his honor."

It is best to use the freshest, small Brussels sprouts for this recipe since the larger ones tend to be too chewy and tough to eat. These have a good strong flavor and make a great snack or addition to a holiday pickle platter.

BILL TERRY'S PICKLED BRUSSELS SPROUTS

MAKES 2 PINTS (OR 1 QUART)

15 to 20 Brussels sprouts, about
   3 pounds, tough outer leaves
   removed
10 cups water
1 cup coarse salt (kosher or
   pickling)
5 cups distilled white vinegar
2 tablespoons white mustard seed
2 tablespoons whole cloves
2 tablespoons black peppercorns
2 tablespoons sugar
10 small red chili peppers

Wash the Brussels sprouts under cold running water and trim the stems close to the bottom of each sprout, but not too close or the sprouts will fall apart. Cut an X into the base of each, then place the sprouts in a large, nonreactive bowl.

Bring the water to a boil in a large, nonreactive pot, add the salt, and stir until it dissolves. Pour the solution over the sprouts and submerge them by covering with a plate that can fit inside the bowl. Cover with a clean dish towel and set aside for 24 hours.

When the Brussels sprouts have almost finished soaking, sterilize the jars and lids according to the directions on pages 12–14. In another large, nonreactive bowl, mix together the vinegar, mustard seed, cloves, peppercorns, sugar, and chili peppers to create a brine. Drain the Brussels sprouts in a colander, pack them into the jars, and add the brine to completely cover, leaving a ¼ inch free at the top of the jar. Screw on the lids. Process the jars in a hot-water bath for 10 minutes to seal. Allow the jars to cool, then store in a cupboard for 3 weeks for the flavor to fully develop. Sealed, the sprouts will last up to 1 year. Refrigerate after opening.

_B_ack home in Japan," says Nikki Rossi, "homemade pickles have become quite rare, although commercially packaged pickles are sold in abundance in Japanese supermarkets. You can find a greater variety of vegetables there than in the United States, as well as a strong pickling tradition and many different pickling methods."

When Nikki was young, her grandmother made pickles at home. Her dad, who was raised in the northernmost island of Hokkaido, couldn't stand the flavor of pickles, so her mom rarely made them. She liked them, though, and misses the taste. In Connecticut, when Nikki's shiso plants bear leaves (see page 21), she'll pickle them in salt to serve with rice. In the recipe that follows, Nikki pickles *hakusai,* or a Chinese cabbage known as napa cabbage in the United States; this is a popular dish in Japan.

HAKUSAI-ZUKE
(Napa Cabbage with Kelp and Chilies)

MAKES 4 SMALL SERVINGS

1 large head *hakusai* or napa
   cabbage cut in quarters
   lengthwise, washed and drained
One 10-inch piece dried kelp,
   broken into 2-inch pieces
⅓ cup coarse salt (kosher or
   pickling)
4 dried red chili peppers

Set the quarters of cabbage, heart-sides out, in direct sunlight for 1 to 2 days; they will wilt more than they'll dry out.

In a large, nonreactive bowl, layer the cabbage with the salt, kelp, and chilies, making sure that some salt falls in between the layers of cabbage. Top with a plate that can fit inside the bowl and add a heavy weight (a brick or large can of beans will work). Let stand for 2 to 3 days in a shady, indoor place, away from direct light or heat.

After the third day, reduce the weight by half and let the cabbage stand 4 to 5 more days, until it's tender but still crunchy. It will keep up to 3 weeks before spoiling.

When you're ready to serve, stack the cabbage leaves and softened kelp and cut them into 2-inch-thick slices. Place in individual serving bowls, discarding the chilies and any discolored cabbage roots.

This recipe is another one from Jacqueline Newman, (see also pages 33, 87, 97, 114, 115, and 135) and despite its name, it's neither too hot nor too sour. In fact, to my chili-loving taste buds it was mild. I used low-sodium soy sauce with good results. This recipe didn't seem like a pickle to me until I allowed it to sit for an hour so the juices could leech from the cabbage. Serve this dish cold with rice, meat, or smoked tofu for a healthy meal or snack.

HOT AND SOUR PICKLED CABBAGE

MAKES 3 CUPS

¼ cup corn oil
1 head Chinese cabbage, about 2 pounds, cut into 1-inch-wide pieces, washed and drained
4 dried red chili peppers, seeded and cut into thin strips
1 tablespoon Sichuan peppercorns (see page 21)
3 tablespoons soy sauce, preferably the low-sodium variety, thinned with 2 teaspoons water
2 tablespoons black vinegar (see page 22)
2 tablespoons sugar
1 teaspoon coarse salt (kosher or pickling)
2 tablespoons dark sesame oil

Heat the corn oil in a large skillet or wok, then add the cabbage and chili peppers and sauté over medium-high heat for 1 minute. Add the Sichuan peppercorns, soy sauce, vinegar, sugar, and salt and sauté for another 2 minutes, stirring constantly with a wooden spoon.

Remove the skillet from the heat, transfer the cabbage mixture to a serving bowl, and refrigerate for 1 hour. Add the sesame oil, stir, and serve cold or refrigerate for up to 2 days.

The Mott Street Senior Center is a recreational center in New York City for the elder generation. Located where Little Italy meets Chinatown, it reflects the communities' culturally diverse population. Many who live here were born in China. They gather to sing songs, make crafts, learn about modern health and nutrition, and eat meals with their peers. There are social workers on hand to direct the activities and address the needs of the community.

Huikang Cheung, a retired woman who visits at the center, trained and worked as a nurse in the Canton region of China. After leaving the medical profession behind to move to New York City, she took a job as a cook at China Patiwan, a Chinese restaurant once located in Manhattan. She worked there for more than twelve years, and often made pickles at the restaurant.

Although her recipe for pickled cabbage may not taste or even look pickled, it *is*. The bok choy retains its crunchy texture, but it tastes like it has been cooked. Serve cold when you want a side dish of fresh-tasting leafy greens with a kick. Any kind of Chinese cabbage is suitable.

PICKLED CHINESE CABBAGE
(Bok Choy)

MAKES 3 CUPS

1 head bok choy or other Chinese cabbage, about 2 pounds
1 tablespoon coarse salt (kosher or pickling)
1 tablespoon sugar
2 tablespoons dark sesame oil
2 teaspoons cayenne pepper

Cut the cabbage into long, thin strips and place in a large, nonreactive bowl. Sprinkle the salt all over the cabbage. Cover with a plate that's small enough to fit into the bowl, and top with a heavy weight (a brick or a can of beans will work). Let stand 12 hours or overnight.

In the morning, drain the cabbage, return it to the bowl, and add the sugar, tossing to combine.

Put the sesame oil in a small sauté pan over medium heat, and when it's hot, add the cayenne and stir for 1 minute; be sure not to burn the pepper. Pour the seasoned oil over the cabbage and toss to combine. Let the cabbage sit for at least 2 hours before eating. Store in the refrigerator for up to 1 week.

This is probably my favorite recipe for kimchi. It's unconventional in that it contains beef stock. The uniform layers of spongy napa cabbage are fun to pick apart and eat using chopsticks. To truly savor the many dimensions of this kimchi, eat it alone or with rice, for a small meal or midday snack.

"I studied with a French chef for the last five years," says Young S. Choi, owner of the Woo Lae Oak restaurant. "For my kimchi, I just reduce some traditional ingredients and put other things in instead. The taste is more mild, and the smell not as strong as that of traditional kimchi. In Korea we have many, many kinds of kimchi—more than one hundred varieties. All families seem to have a different recipe. It is eaten like bread with butter.

"I have three kimchi recipes that are the most popular dishes at the restaurant. This pickled napa cabbage is the most famous. This recipe is mine—the Woo Lae Oak style. It soaks overnight to make sure it gets crisp, not chewy. Another is cucumber kimchi (see page 35). The other is made with daikon radish (see page 88). We also do *Ma Nel Jang a Chi* (pickled garlic).

"There is a big Korean community in Flushing, Queens, and a big Korean community out in New Jersey, so getting the necessary produce is much easier than it was twenty years ago. Not long ago, if you wanted to make kimchi, you would have to travel half an hour to get the right cabbages.

"The vessel that kimchi is made in depends on the family. Some families use a huge clay jar. A long time ago, we didn't have refrigeration. We put the jar underground or in a cool, dark place and weighed the contents down with a heavy stone. My mother put something heavy on top.

"It still takes a lot of energy to make kimchi. Here at the restaurant, we have one woman who makes the kimchi 365 days a year. It's not like making salad where you chop it up and put dressing on top. Kimchi involves so many more procedures. You want to minimize evaporation because the salt tends to dry out the kimchi. If it does dehydrate, Koreans always recycle it and use it another way. If it's too sour, they chop it and make *Kimchi Chi Gi* (a casserole).

"I travel to a lot of countries and they all have pickles, too—cucumber, tomato—so many pickles in the world! In Korea kimchi is served at every meal.

On our menu at Woo Lae Oak, we have *Bin Dae Duk* (a pancake made of mung bean, kimchi, scallions, and bean sprouts), *Kimchi Mandu* (sautéed beef and kimchi dumplings), *Kimchi Chi Ge* (kimchi, vegetable, and pork casserole), and *Bok Kum Bap* (fried rice with your choice of kimchi or vegetables)."

BAE CHU KIMCHI
(Napa Cabbage Kimchi)

MAKES 1 GALLON

4 heads napa cabbage, about
   7 to 8 pounds, washed and
   drained
4¼ cups plus 1½ tablespoons
   coarse kosher salt
1 daikon radish, puréed
1 medium onion, peeled and puréed
¾ cup chopped scallions (about
   2 bunches)
3 or 4 red chili peppers, to taste,
   cored, seeded, and puréed
½ cup pureed garlic
2 tablespoons puréed fresh ginger
8 tablespoons fish sauce (see page
   19)
½ cup beef stock, preferably
   homemade

Put the whole cabbages in a kimchi pot or pickling crock and pour 4½ cups of the salt over the cabbage cover and let stand for 12 hours or overnight. In the morning, rinse off the salt with cold running water and drain the cabbages in a colander for 30 minutes. Cut the cabbages in half lengthwise.

In a mixing bowl, combine the remaining ingredients with the 1½ tablespoons salt. Mix well until a coarse paste is formed. Spread the seasoning paste between the cabbage leaves, making sure each of the leaves is coated, and then stack the cabbage halves in the kimchi pot and cover. Let stand at room temperature for 1 day, then refrigerate to chill before serving. Refrigerated, it will last for 2 weeks.

*O**f all the wonderful homemade** dishes Luyben Tachev remembers eating while growing up in Bulgaria, this is the only one that he can remember how to make. He prepares this very simple appetizer three to four times a year, and eats it along with a small glass of vodka.

When Luyben was a child, his father used to fill a large wooden barrel with cabbages, pour "a lot of salt" over them, and then completely cover them with fresh spring water. Every day, for a few weeks, he would drain the brine out through a spigot located at the bottom of the barrel, but then immediately pour the same brine over the cabbages. According to Luyben, this was done to maintain an even amount of salt throughout the barrel; the salt crystals naturally fell to the bottom.

SALTED CABBAGE

MAKES 8 SMALL SERVINGS

1 large head green cabbage, about
2½ pounds, cut into eighths,
  washed and drained
7 tablespoon coarse salt (kosher or
  pickling)
8 cups spring water, or more to
  cover
1 small onion, chopped (optional)
Sprinkle of paprika (optional)

Place the sections of cabbage and the salt in a large, nonreactive bowl. Toss to distribute the salt and add the spring water to cover. Top with a plate that's small enough to fit in the bowl and add a heavy weight (such as a brick or large can of beans), so the cabbage is completely submerged.

Every morning for 4 days, remove the cabbage and pour the brine into a clean pitcher. Immediately replace the cabbage, and pour the brine back into the bowl. Each time, put the plate and the weight on top of the cabbage.

When the cabbage is ready to serve, fork small portions into bowls and garnish with the onion and paprika, if desired. The salted cabbage can be stored at room temperature for several weeks.

*A*ccording to *Michael Born,* who came to the United States from Latvia almost twenty years ago, there are two secrets to this recipe's success: first, it must be made during a full moon in order for the dish to turn out right. The second secret is fresh pomegranate juice.

"This recipe originated in the Caucacus Mountain region, where it was made by Georgian Armenians in Banjani," explains Michael. "I use pomegranate juice for flavor and the peel for coloration, but in some regions they use sweet beet for taste and color instead. In Ukrainian and Baltic states like Latvia (White Russia), they always start to pickle the cabbage on a full moon. That way, the crispiness stays and it has a 'full' taste. I don't know if you can prove this superstition, but it works. And if it works, don't change it! This cabbage can stay fresh and crunchy for three or four months, a most important fact during the long winter months.

"There's not much vinegar used in this recipe; I use red wine that's too old for drinking instead of throwing it away. The best wine to use is a Georgian wine called Telavi or Teliani that's made from the Rkatsiteli and Cabernet grape varieties.

"The last time I made this cabbage was in January—on a full moon, of course. But I integrated American ingredients and added orange juice. The result was amazing. Even the old-time Russian traditionalists, when they tasted it, they said, 'Hey that's not bad.' And they asked me, 'How do you do this?' and I said 'Orange juice.' And they said, 'You're kidding me. Orange juice and old Russian cabbages!'"

When buying fresh pomegranates, choose ones heavy for their size with a bright color and blemish-free skin. Use the peel only for coloration, discard it when you're ready to eat the cabbage. I made this recipe with bottled juice because fresh pomegranates, which are grown throughout Asia, the Mediterranean, and California, were not in season. In North America, they are usually available in October and November. The bottled juice was an acceptable, although inferior, substitute for fresh juice.

The most important thing is to be creative, just like Michael was. Try cranberry and orange juice mixed together as a substitute for the pomegranate. It will preserve the beautiful color, if not the taste.

(continued on next page)

FULL-MOON CABBAGE WITH FRESH POMEGRANATE JUICE

1 head white cabbage, about 2½
    pounds, cut into quarters, washed
    and drained
1 teaspoon black peppercorns
4 to 5 sprigs fresh parsley, including
    stems
2 bay leaves
⅓ cup coarse salt (kosher or
    pickling)
5 cups strong red wine vinegar
    or red wine that's too old for
    drinking
2½ pomegranates (enough for 1 cup
    juice, see Note)
2 cups water

Fill a large pot with water, add the cabbage, and bring to a boil. Simmer until just tender, 20 to 35 minutes. Drain in a colander and rinse under cold running water until cool. Place the cabbage quarters inside a 1-gallon jar sterilized according to the directions on pages 12–14. Add the parsley, bay leaves, peppercorns, and pomegranate.

In a mixing bowl, combine the salt vinegar, juice, and water, stirring until the salt until dissolved.

Pour the brine over the cabbage and screw on the lid. Place the jar in a cool, dark place for 4 days and the cabbage is ready to serve. Refrigerated, it will keep for 3 weeks.

Note: To make the pomegranate juice, cut the pomegranates into quarters and scoop the kernals into a blender. Discard the connective membrance that holds the kernals together, but save the thin red outer peel to add extra color to your brine. Pulse the kernals until liquified, then strain through a fine-mesh sieve to the remove the pulp and seeds.

$\mathcal{E}$*ddie and Lee Ann Jacobian* run The Pickle People in West Hempstead, Long Island (for more of their story, see page 79). They are part of a pickle legacy that can be traced to Armenia, where Eddie's mother, Alice Apkarian, learned the art of pickling as a child. Her story includes the tale of a grapevine the family brought to America from Armenia and planted in the yard of their first house in Queens, where it continues to thrive today.

Lee Ann Jacobian, Alice's daughter-in-law, tells us that Alice grew up in Manhattan during the 1930s. She had two sisters and a brother. Her mother, Madeleine Dikranian, was from Armenia, at that time a part of Russia. Alice remembers that her mother always had a small grape-leaf plant "brought over from the other side," which she kept in a flowerpot.

It never got big enough for pickling leaves while it was in the pot. But every Sunday, Alice and her family would pack a picnic and take the long subway ride to Van Cortlandt Park in the Bronx, where grapes grew wild in the woods. The whole family would bring large bags, which they would fill with the grape leaves. Alice said the only problem was that poison ivy also grew among the grapevines; because of this, her mother brought brown soap and everyone had to wash up in a nearby stream.

Alice Akparian and family picking grape leaves in Cortland Park. Photo courtesy of Lee Ann Jacobian.

Once home, each child had the job of putting the leaves together in small bunches, then rolling and tying them with a string. Meanwhile, her mother would boil salted water on the stove, drop the grape leaves in, then quickly remove them and put them into jars.

When Alice was eleven years old, her family moved to Astoria, Queens. The grape plant "brought over from the other side" was planted, because for the first time in America, they had a backyard. It thrived!

(continued on next page)

When Alice married in 1948, her mother gave her a small cutting from the original grape-leaf plant. She planted it in her new yard and it still grows there today. Alice pickles the leaves from this plant every year, but she has simplified her mother's recipe: She still ties them with string in small bunches, but rather than boiling them, she puts them directly into jars filled with a more salty, cold brine. Both variations are included here.

Use young grape leaves that are available early in the summer; they should be the same shade of green on each side. Late season leaves will have a tough, fiberous, light-brown underside that is undesirable.

MADELEINE DIKRANIAN'S TRADITIONAL PICKLED GRAPE LEAVES

MAKES 1 QUART (10 BUNDLES)

**80 fresh grape leaves, gathered
 from the vine
2 quarts water
½ cup coarse salt (kosher or
 pickling)**

Wash the leaves under cold running water, removing tough stems; stack them together, 8 to 10 leaves thick, and roll them like a cigar. Tie each roll securely with cotton twine or kitchen string.

Put the water and salt in a large, nonreactive pot and bring to a boil over medium-high heat. Gently place the grape-leaf bundles in the boiling water, one at a time (you can use tongs), removing each after just blanched (about 1minute), and transferring them to paper towels to drain. Reserve the salted water to use as a brine.

While the grape leaves cool, sterilize the jar and lid according to the directions on pages 12–14. Pack the grape-leaf bundles into the 1-quart jar, pour the salted water over the bundles to cover, and tightly screw on the lids.

Let stand for 12 hours or overnight. Refrigerated, the grape leaves will last 2 to 3 months.

ALICE APKARIAN'S "LIKE I DO" PICKLED GRAPE LEAVES

**80 fresh grape leaves, gathered
from the vine**
2 quarts cold water
**¾ cup coarse salt (kosher or
pickling)**

Wash the leaves under cold running water, removing tough stems; stack them together, 8 to 10 leaves thick, and roll them like a cigar. Tie each roll securely with cotton twine of kitchen string.

Sterilize the jar and lid according to the directions on pages 12–14. Mix the cold water and salt in a large, nonreactive bowl. Pack the grape-leaf bundles into the 1-quart jar, pour the salted water over the bundles to cover, and tightly screw on the lids.

Let stand for 12 hours or overnight. Refrigerated, the grape leaves will last 2 to 3 months.

CHAPTER THREE

Root
Vegetables

WE HAVE BEEN ENJOYING A ROOT VEGETABLES RENAISSANCE IN recent years. It's exciting since root vegetables—the quintessential peasant food—were once regarded as low-status foods, literally devalued because they grew under the earth.

Over the last twenty years or so, America's fascination with fresh and seasonal ingredients has grown, leading many cooks to seek unusual vegetables to experiment with in their gardens and kitchens. From radishes to rutabagas, roots are immensely diverse in size and color, in raw and cooked texture, and in their flavor. They are delicate enough for summer dishes and hearty enough to be included in winter ones.

The recipes that follow feature the less starchy root vegetables, which are ideal for pickling. They retain their shape and their color becomes more vivid, when pickled. Better still their flavors are perfectly complemented by the spices, vinegars, and sugars used in the pickling process. Pickled beets are my personal favorites. However, every recipe in this chapter differs greatly from the next, just like the unique people who created them.

---

*W*hile delivering my Grandma's eulogy, the pastor of her church, Vernon Percival, mentioned that he would surely miss her pickled beets. Those beets were famous; I could hear people begin to giggle through their tears. The beet pickles symbolized everything good about Grandma. Of the many things she did right, what suddenly stood out most in all its vibrancy of color, texture, and sweet tartness, was a jar of pickled beets.

A few years ago, I planted beets in my backyard in Brooklyn. I had never loved their taste, but I planted them because they reminded me of Grandma. And they grew! From my small garden alone, I was able to can 3 pints of beet

On the previous spread: From left are Lift *(Turnips Colored with Beet Juice, page 91),* Gourmet Garden's Dilled Carrot Spears *(page 93),* Kai Du Ki *(Daikon Radish Kimchi, page 88), and* Pickled Ginger *(page 89) along with fresh beets, ginger root, and a variety of turnips.*

pickles using a recipe from Linda Ziedrich's *The Joy of Pickling*. It was my first solo pickling experiment and all three jars sealed beautifully. I mailed a jar to each of my parents in Texas so they could taste-test, and saved the last for my pickle plate at Thanksgiving. My mom thought Grandma's beets had a different texture, but she said mine tasted okay (she's not too fond of beets). My dad ate the whole jar in one sitting.

My aunt gave this recipe to my grandmother back in the 1950s. Essentially they are my grandma's since this is what she is known for, but it was probably passed up to her from Aunt Judy's mother-in-law who, unfortunately, I did not know. I like these beets as part of the Thanksgiving and Christmas relish tray, as well as in green salads with blue cheese and walnuts.

BEET PICKLES

MAKES 4 PINTS

15 to 18 small to medium red beets
2 cups sugar
2 cups distilled white vinegar
2 cups water
1 tablespoon ground cinnamon, or
   1 cinnamon stick
1 teaspoon whole cloves,
   4 to 5 buds
1 teaspoon allspice

Cut off the beet greens, if any, leaving 1 inch of stem attached to each beet, then scrub the beets under cold running water. Fill a large pot with water, immerse the beets, and bring to boil over medium-high heat. Cook until tender, about 5 minutes. Drain the beets and, under cold running water, slide off the skins and softened root stems and discard. Slice or quarter the beets to uniform size and set aside in a large, nonreactive pot.

In a separate saucepan over medium-high heat, combine the sugar, vinegar, and water. Wrap the cinnamon, cloves, and alspice in cheesecloth, tie with kitchen twine, and add the spice bag. When the mixture boils, remove the spice bag, stir to make sure the sugar has dissolved, and pour the brine over the beets. Simmer together for 15 minutes, or until tender when pierced with a fork.

Meanwhile, sterilize the jars and lids according to the directions on pages 12–14. Fill the pint-sized jars with the beets and brine, then process for 10 to 12 minutes in a hot-water bath to seal. Allow to cool.

Store the sealed jars at room temperature for at least 3 weeks to allow the flavors to develop. Sealed, the jars will keep for up to 1 year. After opening, refrigerate for up to 6 months.

Jane Wilson Morton has loved the flavor of pickles as far back as she can remember. Her mother once put mustard on her baby bottle nipple to wean her away from it and she said, "More."

Jane's family used to own a delicatessen called Werth and O'Brien at 1130 Flatbush Avenue and Clarendon in Brooklyn, New York. Every time she walked into the store, she would head for the trays of loose pickles arrayed behind the counter. Her favorites were the mustard pickles—and you don't see them around much anymore. She still has the recipe for the pickled beets they made at the store.

These beet pickles are easy and quick to make. I prefer to let them absorb the flavor for at least three days before eating. These beets are great on salads or as a more colorful and sweet pickle on a cheese sandwich.

Willie Lasson, Uncle Frank O'Brien, and Uncle Otto Werth at the Werth and O'Brien Deli. Photo courtesy of Jane Wilson Morton.

WERTH AND O'BRIEN'S PICKLED BEETS

MAKES 4 SMALL SERVINGS

One 16-ounce jar or can sliced beets, drained; or 1½ to 2 cups cooked sliced beets
½ cup distilled white vinegar
¼ cup water
¼ cup dark brown sugar
2 tablespoons sugar
1 tablespoon pickling spice, tied in a cheesecloth spice bag

Place the beets in a glass bowl and set aside.

Put the vinegar, water, brown sugar, granulated sugar, and spice bag in a saucepan over medium-high heat, mix well, and bring to a boil over high heat. Lower the heat to medium and simmer for about 10 minutes, stirring occasionally with a wooden spoon, until a thin syrup forms.

Pour the syrup over the sliced beets, toss to combine, and let cool completely. Cover and refrigerate. Remove the spice bag before serving.

This recipe is best if made a day before so that the beets have time to absorb the flavors.

Variation: Jane likes to add thin rings of red onion to the beet mixture as it cools, although that is not part of the store's original recipe.

A*t first, this pickle* (from a recipe given to me by Jacqueline Newman, see also pages 33, 72, 97, 114, 115, and 135), has a heavy rice wine flavor, but then it mellows as it cools in the refrigerator. It is very refreshing served with hot dishes still steaming from the kitchen stove.

SMASHED RADISH PICKLES

MAKES 1 1/2 CUP

5 to 7 small- to medium
   red radishes (1 bunch), washed
   and drained both ends trimmed
1 small daikon radish, washed
   peeled, and cut into 1-inch cubes
1 teaspoon coarse salt (kosher
   or pickling)
1 tablespoon brown sugar
2 tablespoons rice vinegar
1 tablespoon sesame oil
1 tablespoon corn oil

Smash each radish with the side of a cleaver, then smash the radish pieces to create a pulp. Transfer to a nonreactive bowl, sprinkle with the salt, and let stand in the refrigerator for 30 minutes.

Drain the radishes in a colander, then transfer them to a clean, nonreactive bowl. Add the brown sugar and rice wine and mix well.

In a small pan, heat the sesame oil with the corn oil over low heat. Pour the oil mixture over the radish mixture and toss well to combine. Serve immediately, at room temperature.

This is another of Young Choi's recipes from Woo Lae Oak Restaurant (see page 75 for more about Young). The water from the daikon root leeches out, moistening the pasty consistency of the spices. The flavor is pungent and spicy, yet refreshing and crisp.

KAK DU KI
(Daikon Radish Kimchi)

MAKES 1 PINT

3 daikon radishes, about 3 pounds total, washed, peeled, and cut into ¾-inch cubes
5 scallions, finely chopped
⅔ cup coarse salt (kosher or pickling)
½ cup cayenne pepper
1 tablespoon saccharin, like Sweet 'n Low
1 tablespoon fish sauce (see page 19)
1½ tablespoons peeled and crushed or finely grated garlic
1 tablespoon peeled and crushed or finely grated fresh ginger

Put all the ingredients together in a large, nonreactive bowl and mix well to combine. Transfer to a kimchi pot or pickling crock, cover, and let stand at room temperature for 1 day. Refrigerate for 2 more days and it's ready to eat.

Serve chilled. Refrigerated, this kimchi will last up to 2 weeks.

M**adege **Kho gave me delicious Filipino pickle recipes
that are closely tied to her memories of life back in the northern Philippines.
(For more, see pages 90, 124, and 145.) Madge says this pickled ginger is easy
to assemble. Use it in stir fries and dipping sauces in place of fresh ginger,
throw it into salads, or eat it with sushi. Just remember, as with all the recipes
in this book, a little goes a long way. Like the others, this recipe can be multi-
plied to accommodate your needs.

MADGE KHO'S PICKLED GINGER

MAKES 1 CUP

1 cup rice vinegar
⅔ cup sugar
One 4- to 5-inch piece fresh ginger,
   about 3 ounces, peeled and sliced
   paper-thin with a mandoline or
   knife

Put the vinegar and sugar in a
saucepan over low heat and stir
until the sugar dissolves. Remove
the pan from the heat and set aside
to cool.

Meanwhile, sterilize a small
glass jar and lid according to the
directions on pages 12–14. Transfer
the ginger and syrup to the jar, leaving at least 2 inches free at the top
of the jar. Screw the lid on tightly.
Let stand at room temperature for
about 1 month; the ginger should
mellow in flavor and turn pink.
Refrigerated, it will last up to 6
months.

"This is so good," Madge Kho says of this recipe. "In the Philippines, I remember a woman who would sell fried chicken from a cart—pickled radish always came with it. I have since learned how to make it myself."

Within a few days, the radish will start to ferment and may smell stinky like kimchi, but don't despair. After a month, it will have a very nice, mellow flavor, but I prefer the radish cut paper thin so I can enjoy it more quickly. This pickle does a very good job at cutting the oily taste of fried foods and can also be eaten as a salad.

MADGE KHO'S PICKLED RADISH

MAKES 4 SMALL SERVINGS

1 large daikon radish, about 1 pound
1¼ tablespoons coarse salt (kosher or pickling)
¾ cup distilled white vinegar
6 tablespoon sugar
¼ teaspoon hot red pepper flakes

Wash the radish, cut off the stem end, and peel. Slice it into paper-thin rounds, ⅛-inch-thick at most (see Note), and transfer to a nonreactive bowl. Add 1 tablespoon of the salt, and using your fingers, gently rub the radish pieces until the salt has covered each piece. Let stand for 15 minutes at room temperature, then rinse the radish under cold running water and drain thoroughly in a colander.

Return the radish to the bowl, add the vinegar, sugar, red pepper flakes, and the remaining ¼ tablespoon salt, and toss gently to combine.

If you use a mandoline to slice the radish paper-thin, you can eat the radish after allowing it to marinate in the refrigerator for just 6 to 8 hours. Sliced normally, it can be eaten after only 3 days, but in either case, the pickled radish will taste best when refrigerated for at least a week and even up to a month. Covered and refrigerated, it will keep for up to 6 months.

If you are lucky enough to live or work near Kalustyan's, the imported food shop on Manhattan's East Side, you are familiar with the array of brightly colored pickles that accompany Arpiar Afarian's beautiful vegetarian sandwiches. I always ask for my sandwiches to be loaded with pickles. The store makes the pickled turnips on site and they are always included with the sandwiches. (*Lift* is pronounced lif-it.) The recipe for another Kalustyan treat—Preserved Lemons—appears on page 126.

LIFT
(Turnips Colored with Beet Juice)

MAKES 1 QUART

2 cups water
6 tablespoons coarse salt (kosher or pickling)
1 small cube French bread or other yeast bread
5 to 6 medium turnips, about 4 pounds, washed, peeled, and cut in ⅛-inch pieces
4 small red beets, left whole, for color
2 to 3 tablespoons fresh lemon juice or cider vinegar

Sterilize the jar and lid according to the directions on pages 12–14. Mix together the water and salt in a nonreactive bowl to make a brine.

Place the bread in the quart-sized jar, and then pack in the turnips and beets. Pour in the brine to cover, but leave at least 2 inches free at the top of the jar. Add the lemon juice to taste and tightly screw on the lid.

In the summer, place the jar outside in a sunny place for 1 week. In colder months, store it close to the heater or oven for 2 weeks. The turnips are ready to eat when they are beet colored throughout and no longer have a raw flavor.

Refrigerated, they will last up to 6 months.

***W**hile visiting family in Texas,* I walked through the stalls at the Dallas Farmers' Market and happened upon a family-run produce stand called Pat's Pea Patch. They had a huge variety of pickles and salsas for sale, and I couldn't make up my mind which one to try (since I had very little space left in my suitcase). I made a quick decision and brought a jar of pickled carrots and a bag of their dried pinto beans and went on my way. Two days later, I was back at the market to talk pickles with Shirley Sherlock, who would eventually put me in touch with her busy son Pat, farmer and owner of the Pea Patch.

A few months later over the telephone, Pat told me that he started farming and picking peas on the farmland he now owns when he was just twelve years old. Twenty-nine years later, in 1995, he bought the farm, located in Canton, Texas, from his aunt. It's a family affair at the farmers' market stall where his mom, brother, cousins, and kids pitch in to rotate work shifts. The pickles, it turns out, are someone else's recipe. "If you want a recipe," Pat advised, "Call Barbara and tell her that I gave you her number; she's nice and will be glad to talk with you."

Enter Barbara Bradshaw, owner of Gourmet Gardens in Rusk, Texas. Barbara started out in business operating a barely surviving "u-pick-it" peach and blueberry farm. Her son, who was studying marketing and economics at Stephen F. Austin State University at the time, convinced her either to create a new business plan or sell the farm. With his vision and her perseverance, she began hand-preserving syrups, salsas, jams, and pickles, eventually packing her goods for other people, such as Pat Sherlock at Pat's Pea Patch. Eleven years later, Gourmet Gardens sells products nationwide, has a web site, and is one of the few FDA-approved, hand-packed food processors in the United States. Barbara operates it with her son and twenty-five other local employees.

Because of the company's success, the United States Director of Trade invited Barbara to represent American commerce on a trip to the Middle East, including Lebanon and Syria. Despite concerns about travel at such a politically delicate time, she intends to carry forth with a uniquely personal commitment. Many years ago, her own family immigrated to America from Syria. Amid troubled times, her grandfather was forced to flea, leaving his family to roam homeless in the Syrian mountains. Seven years later, without much hope of ever finding his family alive, he returned to Syria and, in fact, did find them. As a family, they walked thirty-nine miles, where they boarded a boat and headed west. Barbara intends to visit the same village where her father was born. She will be the first in her family to return.

Both Barbara and Pat say these carrots are not top-sellers, but—as with all Barbara's recipes—they are made the old-fashioned way, "like grandma used to make." Crunchy and just a little hot, these carrot spears are popular with people who use them as drink stirrers. This is a simple recipe that I've adapted from the one shared with me by Barbara, but the result is very tasty and oh-so-colorful. Please make and enjoy.

GOURMET GARDEN'S DILLED CARROT SPEARS

MAKES 4 PINTS

4 cloves garlic, peeled and left whole
4 (1- to 2-inch long) hot red chili peppers
4 sprigs fresh dill
2 pounds carrots, peeled and cut into spears
2½ cups distilled white vinegar
¼ cup coarse salt (kosher or pickling)
2½ cups water

Sterilize the jars and lids according to the directions on pages 12–14. Into each pint-sized jar, place 1 clove of garlic, 1 chili, and 1 sprig dill, then pack the carrot spears vertically into the jars.

Combine the vinegar, salt, and water in a saucepan and bring to a boil over medium-high heat. Pour the hot brine over the carrots, leaving at least ¼ inch free at the top of each jar. Remove the air bubbles, then screw on the lids. Process the jars in a hot-water bath for 10 minutes to seal.

Allow the jars to cool, then store in a cool, dark cupboard for a least 3 weeks before tasting.

Refrigerate after opening, for up to 6 months.

CHAPTER FOUR

Eggplant, Tomatoes, Mushrooms, and More

IT'S IRONIC THAT THIS CHAPTER IS ABOUT PRESERVING A GROUP OF vegetables once considered poisonous. From peppers to mushrooms to tomatoes, all were considered fatal or harmful if eaten. Only in the last few hundred years have these foods been deemed safe for human consumption.

Eggplant is loved all over the world, especially throughout the Mediterranean, from the Near to the Far East. It comes in many varieties, from tiny white "egg" eggplants to the large purple variety widely available across this country. Eggplant flesh is both versatile and satisfying, often substituting for meat in main dishes here and abroad. All eggplant are suitable for pickling.

Okra is one among a variety of foods introduced to American soil by West Africans who were brought to the southern, agriculturally rich states as slaves. The okra crops thrived in the warm climate and became overabundant, so pickling was a great way to preserve the okra pods without intensifying the sliminess often associated with cooked okra. The marvelous pickled okra recipe in this chapter was passed down through the generations from a grandmother to a granddaughter who now carries on the family pickling tradition.

In North America, tomatoes are at their most abundant in the late summer, but the plants continue to bear fruit through early fall. In order to prevent wasting any tomatoes left on the vine, try pickling them. South Asian tomato pickles and chutneys require the fleshier red tomatoes at their peek of ripeness and seasonality. However, even large pink or green tomatoes, sometimes too bitter and hard to eat plain, can make good pickles.

On the previous spread: From far left, front to back, Tasty Eggplant Pickles (page 97), Renuka's Tomato Pickle (pages 101), and Dilly Hot Green- and Wax-Bean Pickle (page 108), amid an array of peppers, beans, eggplants, and pickling spices.

This eggplant pickle is similar in texture to Tuhin Dutta's Indian recipe that follows, but they are completely different in flavor sensation. The soy sauce and vinegar with a small amount of sugar make this pickle extremely enjoyable to eat with any snack or meal. This is another Chinese-inspired recipe of Jacqueline Newman (see pages 33, 72, 87, 114, 115, and 135).

TASTY EGGPLANT PICKLES

MAKES 4 SMALL SERVINGS

4 Japanese eggplants, about
   2 pounds total, peeled and cut
   in half lengthwise
1 teaspoon dark sesame oil
3 tablespoons minced cilantro,
   leaves only
½ teaspoon coarse salt (kosher
   or pickling)
1 teaspoon sugar
6 tablespoons rice vinegar
2 tablespoons soy sauce
1 tablespoon minced or
   grated fresh ginger
1 tablespoon minced or
   grated garlic
1 tablespoon minced or
   grated red pepper

To Serve
1 teaspoon toasted sesame seeds

Line a bamboo steamer with a piece of parchment paper, then take a large cooking fork and punch a few dozen holes in the paper. Place the eggplant halves on the parchment paper, put the lid on the steamer, and steam over rapidly boiling water for about 20 minutes, until tender. Transfer the steamer to the sink, remove the parchment from under the eggplants, and let them drain for 10 minutes. This should eliminate most of the water in the eggplants.

Using a fork, run through the eggplant so it shreds the eggplant meat effectively scooping out the eggplant halves to create long, thin strips. Discard the skins, and transfer the eggplant to a glass serving bowl. Cover and refrigerate for 1 hour.

Combine the rest of the ingredients in a nonreactive bowl and mix well to create a marinade. Toss the marinade with the chilled eggplant strips, cover the bowl, and return to the refrigerator for another hour or two. Top with the toasted sesame seeds and serve with crackers.

Tuhin Dutta has helped open several Indian restaurants in Manhattan. Mr. Dutta was born in India, schooled in the United Kingdom, and now lives in the United States. He is a kind of culinary philosopher, whose passion about India's culinary culture is contagious. In India, especially in the south, pickles are a part of almost every meal, he explains. Spices and other ingredients vary from north to south, coastal and inland. Banjara Restaurant, one of his more recent endeavors, always offers at least two types of pickles on the menu. He does not make the restaurant's pickles himself, but is happy to explain the lore of pickling in India, where quality (and sometimes edibility) is determined by the hand that prepares them.

"I am from the eastern part of India; most of the pickling that I am familiar with is Bihari or Bengali, or from southeast India. Pickling is one of the oldest preservation techniques: It can involve salt or vinegar, as well as sesame or mustard oil, sugar, lemon juice, and spices. There are vegetable, fruit, meat, and fish pickles—many types of pickles!

"In Indian society, there are beliefs regarding the quality of the cooking and the cook's hands. When an Indian chef compliments someone else's cooking in a restaurant, they'll say, 'That chef has a good hand.' It is a major insult to say a cook has a bad hand. Nothing's wrong with the actual hands, but everybody's system reacts differently to food.

"My mother never made many pickles, because to be honest, her pickles were not that good. It's not that my mother is evil, or that she's a bad cook with other things—but when it comes to pickling, she had a bad hand. In my neighborhood, only the woman next door and her youngest daughter could do it properly. That family had four daughters, and none of the others could make pickles. I think there are a lot of differences between family members. Say a doctor has four sons. Out of the four sons, only one may be a doctor. Not all of them are doctors—one may be a jazz musician, or a chef, or something else. It's the same with making pickles. You have the hand for it or you don't."

This pickle is so delicious and full of interesting flavors, textures, and intense spice, it could almost be served as a main course over rice.

BEGUNER ACHAR

(Eggplant Pickle)

MAKES 3 PINTS

1 large eggplant, about 2 pounds,
  cut into ½-inch-thick sticks
1 onion, minced
½ cup mustard oil (see page 20)
½ cup plus 3 teaspoons canola oil
1 tablespoon minced fresh ginger
1 tablespoon minced garlic
2 teaspoons fennel seed
1 tablespoon cumin seed
½ teaspoon nigella or kalongi
  (see page 21)
½ teaspoon brown mustard seed
1½ cups jaggery (see page 20)
  or molasses
½ cup tamarind paste (see
  page 21)
½ cup distilled white vinegar
2 teaspoons water
2 dried red chili peppers
1 tablespoon fresh lemon juice,
  or to taste
2 tablespoons coarse salt (kosher
  or pickling), plus more to taste

Using a mortar and pestle, combine the ginger, garlic, 3 teaspoons canola oil, and 1 teaspoon of the water to make a paste. In a separate bowl, combine the mustard oil and the remaining ½ cup canola oil and set aside.

Combine the eggplant and salt in a large, nonreactive bowl, mixing to distribute the salt evenly. Allow the eggplant to drain in a colander over the sink or a pan for 1 hour, then pat dry with paper towels.

In a large skillet, heat ⅓ cup of the canola oil until hot, then add the eggplant. In a second skillet, heat another ⅓ cup canola oil, then add the onion and sauté. When lightly browned, add the ginger and garlic paste and cook until brown but not burnt. In a third skillet, heat the 2 tablespoons oil, then add the chili peppers, fennel, cumin, nigella, and mustard seed, and the remaining ⅓ cup canola oil and heat until the seeds start to pop.

Pour the seasoned chili oil into the same pan as the onions, then add the vinegar, jaggery, tamarind paste, and lemon juice; season to taste with salt and mix well, until the jaggery has dissolved. Pour over the eggplant and mix well. Adjust the salt and lemon juice to your liking.

Transfer to a pickling crock and tightly cover. Refrigerate for 3 days before serving. The pickled eggplant will keep well for about 1 month, if refrigerated.

S**alvatore **Agrogent** **comes** **from Rocco Multo, Sicily. His mother was an amazing woman, who cooked to suit each of her children's tastes. One child liked their tomato sauce with tomato seeds; another did not. One child liked his bread baked soft, while Sal, the favorite, preferred his crusty. Maria, the only daughter, did not eat cheese (even the smell made her sick), so hers was another taste to please. His mother catered to these various preferences every day, in addition to keeping house and hand-washing clothes and ironing shirts for three sons and a husband: 1) no starch; 2) light starch; and 3) starch on collars and cuffs only. And, yes, they all came home for lunch!

MELANZANE SOTT-OLIO
(Pickled Eggplant in Olive Oil)

MAKES 3 CUPS

1 to 2 large eggplants, about 2½ pounds, peeled, cut in half lengthwise, then into ⅛-inch-thick slices
1 to 2 tablespoons coarse salt (kosher or pickling)
3 cups water
3 cups distilled white vinegar
3 stalks celery, cut into ⅛-inch-thick slices
½ cup olive oil, or more to taste
4 cloves garlic, peeled and thinly sliced
1½ tablespoons dried oregano
Hot red pepper flakes, to taste

Layer the eggplant slices in a colander, sprinkling the salt between each of the layers. Top with a plate small enough to fit in the colander and add a heavy weight (such as a brick or large cans of tomatoes). To extract the bitter juices, let stand at least 30 minutes, or longer if necessary. Rinse off the salt under cold running water, then let the egg- plant drain in the colander again for 5 to 10 minutes or squeeze lightly between paper towels. Set aside.

Combine the water and vinegar in a large, nonreactive pot, add the celery, and bring to a boil. Cover and cook over high heat for 4 to 5 minutes; the celery should still be somewhat crunchy. Add the egg- plant, return to a boil, and cook for about 2 minutes. Transfer the eggplant and celery to the colander, top with the plate and a weight, and drain again, for 8 to 10 minutes.

In a large, nonreactive bowl, layer the eggplant-celery mixture with drizzles of the olive oil, garlic slices, oregano, and red pepper flakes to taste. Repeat until all the mixture has been used. The eggplant should be coated thoroughly with the olive oil; you can leave the ingre- dients layered or stir to combine.

Serve immediately at room temperature or refrigerate, covered, for up to 1 week.

***R**enuka Potluri hails from* Andhra Pradesh, a state in southeast India that is, in her words, famous for creating "the spiciest and the most authentic, very traditional mouth-watering pickles" in all of India.

This recipe is not as sweet as the tomato chutney on page 103. It has the consistency of chunky tomato ketchups, flavored with spices and garlic.

RENUKA'S TOMATO PICKLE

MAKES 4 TO 6 SMALL SERVINGS,
OR ABOUT 1 PINT

1 pound ripe but very firm roma
   tomatoes (see Note)
Juice of ½ lemon (optional)
½ cup olive oil or canola oil
1 teaspoon brown mustard seeds
2 or 3 dried red chili peppers,
   to taste
¼ teaspoon fenugreek seeds
¼ cup peeled garlic cloves
¼ teaspoon powdered asafoetida
   (see page 19)
1 tablespoon cayenne pepper
¼ teaspoon turmeric
¼ teaspoon ground fenugreek
10 to 12 fresh curry leaves, to
   taste (see page 18)
½ teaspoon coarse salt (kosher or
   pickling)

Blanch the tomatoes in boiling water, then peel, seed, and coarsely chop them. Place the tomatoes in a saucepan over medium heat and cook, stirring occasionally, until they become a thick paste the consistency of ketchup. If the tomatoes lack acidity, add the lemon juice. Remove the pan from the heat and set aside.

Heat the oil in a second saucepan over high heat. When the oil is hot, add the mustard seeds, chili peppers, fenugreek seeds, and garlic. Sauté, stirring constantly so the seasonings don't stick to the pan, until the seeds start to pop and the garlic is golden brown, about 3 minutes. Add the asafoetida, cayenne, turmeric, ground fenugreek, and curry leaves, and cook for another minute. Add the tomatoes and salt, stir to combine, and continue cooking for up to 5 minutes. Remove from the heat and let cool completely.

Meanwhile, sterilize the jar and lid according to the directions on pages 12–14. Transfer the tomato pickle to the pint-sized jar, screw on the lid, and refrigerate. It will stay fresh for up to 3 months in the refrigerator.

Note: Although fresh roma tomatoes are ideal, you can use any firm, ripe tomatoes that are in season, except for cherry tomatoes, which have too many seeds.

A**lthough **Shihka Dalal's family is from Bangladesh and she grew up in Calcutta, she has lived in the United States for as many years as she did in India. She is passionate about food and culture, and occasionally teaches about both. A busy professional who makes time to cook for herself on weekends and for her daughters when they are home from college, she rarely has the luxury of spending hours in the kitchen. Thankfully chutneys, including the recipe for tomato chutney offered here, are very quick and easy to make at home.

"My happiest childhood memories always revolve around my grandparents' home in Calcutta. Today, years later, I find that these memories provide me with the psychological armor I need to live in New York. Very often my mind returns to memories involving food, the smells and noises of my grandmother's kitchen. I have spent many hours trying to recreate those dishes for my children and myself, but my diligent efforts to recapture the exact spicing fall far short of my grandmother's and my mother's expertise.

"Many families take great pride in their pickles and pickling recipes, guarding the recipes as closely as family jewels. There is a great deal of folklore concerning the art of pickling and preserving, and many families still take these beliefs very seriously."

This recipe is fun to make. Not only will it fill your kitchen with a beautiful aroma, it is fascinating to watch the tomato transform in texture from a light colored tomato sauce to a deep, dark caramel-like consistency after the sugar is added and it begins to cool. This is a great tasting condiment for just about any food.

SHIHKA'S TOMATO CHUTNEY

1 pound ripe tomatoes
3 cloves garlic, peeled and minced
3½ tablespoons canola oil
3 dried red chili peppers
2 tablespoons brown mustard seeds
1 teaspoon green serrano chili
   pepper, chopped and seeded
¼ teaspoon cayenne or red pepper
   powder
⅛ teaspoon turmeric
½ teaspoon cumin
One ¼-inch piece fresh ginger,
   peeled and grated
1 pinch sea salt
¼ cup fresh lemon or lime juice
½ cup sugar
2 tablespoons chopped cilantro
Small handful raisins or dates,
   (optional)

Blanch the tomatoes in boiling water, then peel, seed, and coarsely chop them. Combine the tomatoes and garlic in a nonreactive bowl and set aside.

In a wok or cast-iron skillet, heat the oil over medium heat. When the oil is hot, add the red chilies and cook until they start to brown, then add the mustard seeds and stir. When the seeds begin to pop, add the tomato and garlic mixture and chopped serrano chili to the wok and cook for about 1 minute. Next add the cayenne, turmeric, and cumin, and cook for about 3 minutes, stirring so the seasonings don't stick to the pan, until the liquid is the consistency of marinara sauce.

Reduce the heat to low. Using your fingers, squeeze in the ginger, discarding the fibrous pulp, and stir in the salt, lemon juice, sugar, cilantro, and raisins, if desired. Adjust seasonings to taste.

Let cool, then transfer the chutney to an airtight container. It will keep for 2 months in the refrigerator, but after a few weeks it will lose some of its sharp, fresh taste.

This relish quickly spoiled me. My tastebuds had grown numb from from eating commercially packed relishes, but when I tasted this I was surprised how fresh and mellow and soft a good relish can be. This is a perfect accompaniment to hot dogs, hamburgers, and sausages.

"Every fall I make green tomato, onion, and pepper relish," says Jane Wilson Morton (see her pickled beet recipe on page 86). "The recipe I follow comes from an old cookbook called Platter Parade, which consists of favorite recipes from the Marine Corps Wives of Camp Le Jeune, North Carolina. I have made it so often that my grandkids call it Oma Jane's Green Tomato Relish. If I can get enough green tomatoes, I still make a batch that gets me through the winter. It's so good on hamburgers and hot dogs."

OMA JANE'S GREEN TOMATO RELISH

MAKES 6 PINTS

12 medium-sized green tomatoes, coarsely chopped
3 small green bell peppers, cored, seeded, and coarsely chopped
1 red bell pepper, cored, seeded, and coarsely chopped
4 medium onions, coarsely chopped
2 cups sugar
2 cups cider vinegar
2 teaspoons celery seed
2 teaspoons coarse salt (kosher or pickling)

In a food processor or blender, grind together the tomatoes, peppers, and onions. Pour into a cheesecloth-lined colander and drain for 1 hour.

Transfer the vegetable mixture to a large, nonreactive pot, and add the sugar, vinegar, celery seed, and salt, stirring to combine. Bring to a boil and continue to cook over medium-high heat for 30 minutes.

While the mixture is cooking, sterilize the jars and lids according to the directions on pages 12–14. Fill the pint-sized jars with the hot relish. Screw on the lids, and process in a hot-water bath for 10 to 15 minutes to seal. Allow the relish to cool before storing in the refrigerator. Sealed, the relish will keep for 1 year.

I *once led a small* tour through the Lower East Side of New York City. One afternoon we stopped at Sammy's Roumanian Steakhouse where they gave us free samples of green peppers similar to these.

Sammy's was tightlipped about their recipe, but the one below, adapted from 1965's *The Complete Book of Pickles and Relishes* by Leonard Louis Levinson, is very similar in taste.

ROMANIAN PICKLED PEPPERS

MAKES 1 QUART

1 cup water
½ teaspoon coarse salt (kosher or pickling)
1 tablespoon brown sugar
5 to 7 whole green bell peppers, about 3 pounds, at room temperature, washed and dried
2 cup distilled white vinegar
½ carrot, cut in quarters lengthwise
1 clove garlic
1 bay leaf
1 small red chili pepper, minced
4 or 5 black peppercorns, to taste

Combine the water, salt, sugar, and vinegar in a large, nonreactive pot and bring to a boil, stirring the sugar and salt dissolve. Set aside to cool.

To skin the peppers, use a chefs' tongs to hold each one against a high flame until the skin blisters, then plunge it into a bowl of cold water and remove the skin with a paring knife. Transfer the peppers to a colander to drain well.

In the meantime, sterilize the jar and lid according to the directions on pages 12–14. Through a slit in the top or side of each pepper, remove the core and the seeds with a paring knife. Pack the still intact peppers into the quart-sized jar, layering them with the carrot pieces, garlic, bay leaf, red chili, and black peppercorns.

When the brine is cool, pour it over the pepper mixture to cover. Screw on the lid and let stand at room temperature for 1 hour before serving. Refrigerated, the pickled peppers will stay fresh for 2 weeks.

𝓙alapeño peppers are inexpensive and incredibly easy to pickle. Instead of buying the mushy canned variety, I make my own at home. In my opinion, nothing accompanies barbecue, or tops hamburgers or nachos, as well as a few pickled jalapeño slices.

As you use up the slices, top off your vinegar with fresh slices. The vinegar stays good for months. I also use pepper vinegar to splash onto pinto beans or my homemade chili.

PICKLED JALAPEÑO SLICES

MAKES 2 PINTS

½ cup water
1½ cups distilled white vinegar
1 teaspoon coarse salt (kosher or pickling)
¼ teaspoon ground cumin
4 cloves garlic, peeled and left whole
8 to 10 large or 20 small jalapeño peppers (about 2 pounds), sliced into thin rings

Combine the water, vinegar, salt, and cumin in a large, nonreactive saucepan and bring to a boil over high heat to create a brine. In the meantime, sterilize the jars and lids according to the directions on pages 12–14.

Place 2 cloves garlic in each jar and fill evenly with the pepper rings. Pour the hot brine over the peppers to cover and screw on the lids.

Process in a hot-water bath for 10 minutes to seal. Let cool before storing in the refrigerator for 1 to 2 weeks, or until the jalapeño slices lose their bright green color. They are then ready to eat.

No one else in Gwinda Anthony's family makes pickles, but they all expect her to bring her pickled okra for important family gatherings. This special recipe is passed down from her grandmother, but never has been written down—until now. She says, "I am not much on measuring, but the last time I made it, it was wonderful." Her Louisiana-born grandmother, Nora Lockett, cooked and prepared food in the same easy-going way. Gwinda hopes that someone in her family will eventually ask how to make the pickled okra, since she thinks it is an important legacy to pass on. Until then, she will keep on canning.

GWINDA ANTHONY'S PICKLED OKRA

MAKES 6 PINTS

3 pounds small, fresh okra, 3 to 3½ inches long each
5 cups water
3 cups distilled white vinegar
¼ cup coarse salt (kosher or pickling)
2 tablespoons sugar
6 cloves garlic, peeled and left whole
6 small red chili peppers
1 tablespoon dill seed

Thoroughly wash the okra under cold running water and drain in a colander. In the meantime, sterilize the jars and lids according to the directions on pages 12–14. Cut off the top half of the stems, then pack the okra, stem side up, in the jars, and set aside.

Combine the water, vinegar, salt, and sugar in a saucepan, and bring to a boil, stirring until the salt and sugar dissolve. To each jar, add one clove garlic, one chili pepper, and a small pinch of the dill seed. Pour the hot brine over the okra to cover, screw on the lids, and process for 15 minutes in a hot-water bath. Let cool.

Store the jars in the cupboard or another cool, dark place for up to 3 weeks before tasting the okra. After opening, the pickled okra can be kept in the refrigerator for up to 6 months.

𝓘 was inspired to make pickled green and wax beans after examining a beautiful, fresh-picked batch at the farmers' market. I couldn't decide on one kind of bean, so I decided to pickle half and half. I prefer to separate the wax from the green beans for aesthetic reasons, but you may choose to mix the colors in the jar. The two colors of beans and the lone red chili pepper makes these jars of pickles particularly pretty. I like spicy, hot flavors, so this recipe is a personal indulgence: Consider making a batch of these as gifts for your "pepper-bellied" friends. They also liven up a *salade niçoise.*

DILLY HOT GREEN- AND WAX-BEAN PICKLE

MAKES 4 PINTS

2 pounds mixed green and wax beans, trimmed, washed and drained
4 cloves garlic, peeled and left whole
4 bunches fresh dill
4 small red chili peppers
2½ cups distilled white vinegar
2½ cups water
¼ cup coarse salt (kosher or pickling)

Sterilize the jars and lids according to the directions on pages 12–14. Beginning with the longest bean pods, pack the beans, stems down, into the hot jars. To each pint, add one clove garlic; one bunch dill, stems down; and one chili pepper.

Combine the vinegar, water, and salt in a saucepan and bring to a boil, stirring until the salt dissolves. Pour the hot brine over the beans, leaving ¼-inch free at the top of each jar. Remove any air bubbles, tightly screw on the lids, and process the jars for 10 minutes in a hot-water bath to seal. Let cool.

Store the jars in a cupboard, or another cool, dark place for 3 weeks before tasting. After opening, the pickled beans can be kept in the refrigerator for up to 6 months.

im Shaw, *a personal chef* and caterer, claims his mother was a lousy cook, but her pickled mushrooms are still his favorite pickle recipe. "I *love* this recipe—one of the few things my mom made well. She was an awful cook. In fact, we called her the Boil-a-Bag Lady. But these pickled mushrooms were amazing! The same brine works well with cauliflower, too."

PICKLED MUSHROOMS

MAKES 1 QUART

1½ pounds (or two 10-ounce packages) small white mushrooms, brushed free of excess dirt, stems removed
½ cup dry white wine
1 cup cider or red wine vinegar
2 tablespoons fresh lemon juice
½ cup olive oil
1 teaspoon coarse salt (kosher or pickling)
1½ teaspoons sugar
2 tablespoons minced onion
½ teaspoon minced garlic
2 bay leaves

Parboil the mushrooms in a large pot of boiling water, then drain them in a colander. Meanwhile, sterilize the jar and lid according to the directions on pages 12–14.

In a nonreactive bowl, whisk together the wine, vinegar, lemon juice, and olive oil, then add the salt, sugar, onion, garlic, and bay leaves, stirring to combine. Pack the mushrooms into the jar, add the brine to cover, and screw on the lid.

Chill in the refrigerator for 24 hours. Bring to room temperature before serving, however, as the olive oil congeals in the cold. Refrigerated, pickled mushrooms will last up to 3 months.

CHAPTER FIVE

Mixed Vegetables

MIXED-VEGETABLE PICKLES WERE BORN FROM THE NEED TO MAKE something edible out of small quantities of a variety of leftover produce. Mixed pickles were what you made when there weren't enough cucumbers for dill pickles, but too many to throw away, and when you had too many radishes and carrots to eat before they spoiled. With the addition off some vinegar, sugar, salt, and spices, you got something similar in spirit to vegetable stew—only pickled.

This chapter celebrates cultural and culinary diversity as shared through food. The recipes demonstrate how a collection of simple raw vegetables (root vegetables, cucumber, cabbages, beans, eggplants, and cauliflower) combined with unique spices, salt, and vinegar can over time lead to a dish that is no longer raw, but is not cooked either. These mixed-pickle recipes, and the people who shared them, have an elusive quality of flavor that escapes a single definition.

––––––––––

I have always eaten pikliz," says Fabienne Volel. "It is so hot, the first time I ate it I had an attack from it. It is that hot! In Haiti hot pepper is eaten with everything. You find some rare Haitians that don't like hot pepper, but hot *pikliz* is served over one of Haiti's most famous pork dish called *griot*— that's boiled pork with vinegar and spices. You roast the pork for a long time in order to break down the fat in the meat. Then you pour the *pikliz* over it—with vegetables like cabbage, onion, and carrots in it—and you let it sit there. Combining the vinegar and the pork creates a surprisingly balanced taste. They complement each other. You can't stop eating it. This particular recipe for *pikliz* is part of being Haitian. It's almost like you can't be Haitian without having this recipe." Fabienne Volel is a registered dietician for a cancer center in New York. Originally from Haiti, Fabienne loves to cook her favorite foods

On the previous spread: From far left, Mississippi Chow-Chow (page 117), American-Style Okra, Cauliflower, Eggplant, Carrots, and String Beans (page 116), with a small bowl of yellow mustard powder and seeds.

from home for her friends (see page 147 for her *Chiquetaille de Morue* or Haitian Salt Cod Pickle recipe). Slicing the green beans lengthwise is the way Fabienne learned from her mother. They can also be chopped into small pieces if you prefer.

At the NY Food Museum's Second Annual Pickle Day, Fabienne served people samples of her homemade *pikliz*. A few days later while grocery shopping in the city's Chelsea neighborhood, I overheard a couple discussing *pikliz,* saying it was the best thing at Pickle Day that year. Like Fabienne says, "you can't stop eating it."

PIKLIZ

MAKES ABOUT 1 GALLON

5 cups shredded green cabbage (from 1 head)
2 carrots, peeled and shredded
⅓ cup green beans, sliced lengthwise into very thin strips
1 onion, cut in half and sliced
8 to 12 mixed green, red, and yellow habanero or Scotch bonnet chili peppers (see Note)
½ cup fresh or frozen green peas (optional)
4 cups distilled white vinegar
1 teaspoon coarse salt (kosher or pickling)

Sterilize a 1-gallon jar and lid according to the directions on pages 12–14. Put all the vegetables in the jar, add the vinegar and salt, and tightly screw on the lid. Shake the jar vigorously to thoroughly mix the ingredients.

Refrigerate the jar for at least 24 hours before serving. Refrigerated, the *pikliz* will last up to 2 months.

Note: Haitians call habanero peppers piment bouk. *Habanero and Scotch bonnet are two of the hottest varieties of chilies, so please wear gloves when handling them, and don't allow anything that has been in contact with the peppers to touch your face or eyes.*

hese Chinese-inspired recipes recipes come from Jacqueline Newman. For more, see pages 33, 72, 87, 97, and 135.

MIHED CHINESE PICKLE

MAKES 3 CUPS

1 carrot, peeled and cut into 2-inch pieces, then into thin strips

1 daikon, peeled and cut into 2-inch pieces, then into thin strips

1 tablespoon coarse salt (kosher or pickling)

2 tablespoons cloud ear mushrooms, soaked in warm water for 20 minutes; then drained and cut into thin slivers

1 ounce cellophane noodles, soaked in warm water for a half hour; drained, and cut into 4-inch pieces

2 stalks celery, cut into 2-inch pieces, then into thin strips

1 teaspoon sugar

¼ cup soy sauce thinned with water

¼ cup white rice vinegar

2 tablespoons dark sesame oil

1 tablespoon powdered mustard

In a nonreactive bowl, mix the carrot and daikon strips with the salt and let stand for 2 hours. Drain any liquid that has formed, then rinse the vegetables under cold running water and drain them again.

Fill a small saucepan with water, bring to boil, then add the mushrooms and simmer for 10 minutes; drain them and set aside. Bring water to boil in another saucepan, add the cellophane noodles, and simmer for 10 minutes; drain the noodles and set them aside. Blanch the celery in boiling water for 30 seconds, then drain, rinse under cold running water, drain again, and set aside.

Mix the sugar, soy sauce, vinegar, sesame oil, and mustard in a serving bowl, stirring until the mustard is thoroughly dissolved. Add all the vegetables, the mushrooms, and cellophane noodles and toss to combine. Serve at room temperature, as you would a salad. This mixed pickle will keep for 1 week if covered and refrigerated.

Variation: You can substitute shiitake mushrooms for cloud ears, but they should be cleaned, stems removed, and well chopped.

PICKLED CARROT, CUCUMBER, AND RADISH STICKS

MAKES 1 QUART

2 tablespoons Sichuan peppercorns
4 tablespoons coarse salt (kosher or pickling)
6 tablespoons rice vinegar
2 small hot red chili peppers, seeded and minced
1 daikon radish, peeled and cut into matchsticks
1 carrot, peeled and cut into matchsticks
1 English (or hothouse) cucumber, cut into matchsticks
1 tablespoon dark sesame oil

Sterilize the jar and lid according to the directions on pages 12–14.

To make a brine, add the Sichuan peppercorns and salt to 8 cups boiling water. Lower the heat, simmer the brine for 5 minutes, and then cool. Add the vinegar, chilies, and the daikon, carrot, and cucumber sticks to the brine, and refrigerate for 2 or 3 days.

Drain the vegetables, reserving the liquid, and add the sesame oil to the vegetable mix. Serve immediately.

The brine can be used for a second batch of pickles before discarding it. Vegetables left in brine without the oil will keep for 1 month if refrigerated.

PAO CAI *(Hot Celery and Cabbage Pickle)*

MAKES 1 QUART

1 pound Chinese cabbage, washed and drained, cut into 1 inch by 2 inch pieces
1 pound celery, washed and drained, cut into 1 inch by 2 inch pieces
1 hot red chili pepper, seeded and finely minced
1 teaspoon sugar
1 teaspoon coarse salt (kosher or pickling)
½ cup rice vinegar
¼ cup corn oil

In a large, nonreactive bowl combine the cabbage, celery, and chili pepper.

In a small, nonreactive bowl, mix the sugar, salt, and vinegar and stir to dissolve. Pour the brine over the vegetables, cover with a plate, and refrigerate for 12 hours or overnight.

The next morning, drain the vegetables and reserve the brine. Heat the oil in a wok or large skillet and sauté the vegetables for 1 minute over medium-high heat, then remove from the heat and set aside for 1 hour.

Drain the vegetables in a colander. Mix the vegetables with the reserved brine and set aside for 1 more hour. Stir well, drain the vegetable mixture one more time before serving.

The Philippines has one of the most culturally mixed cuisines in Southeast Asia. The influences of China, Spain, and other parts of South Asia are apparent, and the flavors of the food vary from city to city.

Tina Yam, jewelry-maker and longtime resident of New York, shared her recipes (see also pages 123) and reminiscences of life in Jolo before political conflicts drove her and her family to leave this island in the southern Philippines.

This recipe originally comes from Tina's friend, Jesusa Bacalan. Tina believes it is a Filipino recipe that's been modified to include vegetables readily available in America, since cauliflower and carrots are only available seasonally in the Philippines, and thus very expensive. Buy the very narrow Japanese or Asian eggplants, not the big fat eggplants used in eggplant parmigiana.

AMERICAN-STYLE OKRA, CAULIFLOWER, EGGPLANT, CARROTS, AND STRING BEANS

MAKES 1 QUART

10 to 13 small okra, rinsed and trimmed
1 medium carrot, peeled and sliced
⅓ cauliflower, cut into florets
1 Japanese eggplant, sliced
15 to 20 string beans, washed, trimmed, and cut into thirds
1½ cups distilled white vinegar
1 cup sugar
1 tablespoon coarse salt (kosher or pickling), or more to taste

Make sure all your vegetables are very dry or else the brine will become diluted with water from the veggies. Microwave the green beans on high for about 3 minutes so that any moisture evaporates. Wipe of any remaining moisture with a paper towel.

In a large saucepan over medium-high heat, combine the vinegar, sugar, and salt and bring to a rolling boil for 2 minutes to create a brine. Add all the vegetables and continue to boil for another 4 minutes. Transfer the mixture to a clean bowl and let cool.

In the meantime, sterilize the jar and lids according to the directions on pages 12–14. Transfer the vegetables and brine to the jar, tightly screw on the lid, and store in the refrigerator. The mixture is ready to serve when cold. Refrigerated, this recipe will last up to 3 months.

*A*ccording to *Mary Katherine Moore*, "Chow-chow is a catchall phrase for a pickle made with cabbage and whatever else the cook cares to add or has on hand." She says she learned this version while in Tupelo, Mississippi, and likes it because it has a sweet-relish flavor.

MISSISSIPPI CHOW-CHOW

MAKES 3 PINTS

1 large, green cabbage, shredded or finely chopped (yields about 8 cups)
⅔ cup finely chopped onions
1 green bell pepper or green chili peppers, chopped (about ⅔ cup)
2 tablespoons coarse salt (kosher or pickling)

For the Brine:
2 cups cider vinegar
2 cups sugar
2 teaspoons powdered mustard
2 teaspoons celery seed
2 teaspoons white mustard seed
2 whole allspice seeds

Put the cabbage, onion, and pepper in a colander, mix well, then sprinkle with the salt. Place the colander in a large bowl and refrigerate for 12 hours or overnight to drain any excess moisture.

The next morning, combine the brine ingredients in a large, nonreactive pot over medium-high heat and simmer for about 10 minutes, stirring frequently, until the sugar has completely dissolved. Add the vegetables and simmer for another 10 minutes, or until the vegetables are tender.

In the meantime, sterilize the jars and lids according to the directions on pages 12–14. Transfer the vegetables and brine to the jars leaving ½ inch free at the top and process in a hot-water bath for 10 to 15 minutes to seal. Let cool.

You can serve the pickles in 2 weeks or store the jars, sealed, in the refrigerator for up to 1 year.

CHAPTER SIX

Fruit

From musky summer melons to crispy sweet fall apples, fruits keep us anxious for seasonal change. As one season ends, we look forward to the next season's gifts while we wonder what to do with all the still uneaten fruit about to disappear from the market and garden.

Cooking is the most common way to preserve many types of fruit, as heat renders the pectin and natural sugars that act as preservatives. Fruit pickles differ from preserves or jams in that they are meant to be savory. Perhaps pickling fruit is less common because the vinegar contrasts so strongly with the sweetness of the raw fruit, but hard and stone fruits, citrus, melons, and some berries make wonderful pickles. Salting extracts the juice from the fruit and cooking or fermenting softens hard and bitter peels. This is especially true of preserved lemons (page 126), a delicious pickled fruit that lasts for as long as a year in the refrigerator.

Among common and uncommon recipes for fruit pickles in this chapter are several meant to be eaten by themselves rather than as accompaniments. The watermelon pickles (page 127) tangled with fresh dill and celery have a flavor reminiscent of the salty pickled slices I knew as a child in Texas—only their flavor is richer and more interesting. Fruit pickles like the chutney recipe on page 129, are meant to be eaten with meat dishes. In recent years, I have come to adore the highly complementary combination of fruit and meat and recommend that you try this delicious food pairing.

On the previous spread: From left, Spiced Pickled Cantaloupe (page 131), Atchara (Pickled Green Papaya, page 124), Pickled Watermelon with Dill (page 127), and a selection of melons perfect for pickling. A fresh green papaya is shown at far right.

When I told **Annapurna Potluri** I was interested in Indian pickle recipes for this book, her face lit up. I had obviously asked the right person! Her mother, Renuka, is somewhat of a legend in her family for her pickles and she is known by her friends as one of the only people who goes through the trouble to make pickles the old-fashioned way. Renuka says hers aren't as good as the ones her own mother and grandmother made. These are some humble pickles! It makes your mouth water just thinking about it.

True green or sour mangoes may be hard to find. South and Southeast Asian produce stands may carry them seasonally or special order them for you. I found mine in July at a street stall in New York's Chinatown. Do not use unripe yellow mango for this recipe—it doesn't work. Granny Smith apples or crabapples, both quite sour, are suitable substitutions.

Renuka explains, "One can practically live on pickles and rice—at least I can. I have been in the United States for twenty-two years, and the one thing I miss the most is my mom's mango pickle. It is simply the best. Most Indian pickles are made in the summer months, but mango pickle is traditionally made between the last week of April and the first two or three weeks of May each year.

"My fondest memory about mango pickles comes from when I was a young child when my mother would spend weeks looking for the top-quality, freshest ingredients from the most recent crop. Then all those ingredients were carefully prepared for the pickle. The kitchen help would grind cayenne from dried red chili peppers. She would order a few gallons of refined sesame seed oil, which is the only oil used to make the best pickles in most households even to this day.

"My parents owned a mango orchard, so the mangoes for our pickle came from there. They were carefully hand-selected for firmness. When the pickle was finally made, the house smelled like heaven for weeks. I miss a lot of things about India, but what I miss most is my beloved mother, my beautiful sister, and my wonderful brothers, and all my kind relatives and friends. And last, but certainly by no means least, I miss my mom's mango pickle!"

Once you've tasted the homemade version of mango pickles you will be reluctant to return to the jarred supermarket brands. This fresh tasting complex pickle is outstanding.

(continued on next page)

RENUKA'S MANGO PICKLE

MAKES 3 TO 4 PINTS

2 to 3 green and very firm
  mangoes, or Granny Smith apples,
  or crabapples (enough to yield
  4 cups), peeled
1 cup coarse salt (kosher or pickling)
1 cup cayenne pepper
1 cup brown mustard seeds, freshly
  ground to a fine powder
  (see Note)
1 teaspoon turmeric
1 teaspoon fenugreek seeds
¼ cup garlic cloves, peeled and
  left whole
3 cups canola oil

Wash the mangoes in lukewarm water and dry thoroughly with paper towels. Using a very sharp knife, halve each mango, cutting through the pits. Do not remove the hard outer layer that encloses the inside, but remove and discard the seed that is located inside each pit. Cut the flesh into 1-inch cubes and transfer the mango and pits to a large, nonreactive bowl.

In a separate large bowl mix spices and oil together. In a large, nonreactive bowl combine the mangoes and spice mixture and mix well. Cover with a plate and let stand on the counter at room temperature for 2 to 3 days. When it's ready, the pieces attached to the pit will be firm and crunchy.

On the third day, sterilize the jars and lids according to the directions on pages 12–14. Mix the mango well and then spoon pint-sized jars and tightly screw on the lids. Refrigerated, the mango pickle will last up to 6 months. Serve with rice or bread.

Note: Use a clean coffee grinder to grind the seeds to a fine powder.

I **first tasted this pickled mango** in my godmother's home in Jolo, Sulu, in the Philippines, during the late sixties or early seventies when I became her neighbor," Tina Yam recalls (for another recipe from Tina, see page 116). "Ninang Charito, as I called her, often served this as an appetizer or just to snack on. Television was not available (and still is not) in Jolo, so visiting after dinner, or just taking a stroll around the compound was a big part of our social life. Some homeowners would be sitting on their porch or veranda for conversation, often followed by invitations to come in and visit. Homemade munchies, or *chit-chi-rias,* would be served, along with beer, soda, or other beverages. It was a point of pride for homeowners to serve something different. Recipes were often exchanged then modified. By 9:00 P.M., it was time to be in bed."

The tiny Philippine or Carabau green mangoes (about 2 inches in diameter) used in this recipe are currently impossible to find in North America. If you live near a Filipino or Southeast Asian produce dealer, you may be able to coerce a special order during the early summer season. Instead, I used the very firm and bitter 1 to 2 pound green mango (which is difficult to find, but not impossible), chopped into 1-inch cubes. It worked fine. Prepare this recipe at least 2 days before serving

GREEN MANGO CHIT-CHI-RIAS

MAKES 1 QUART

12 to 14 tiny green mangoes,
   2 pounds total, pit removed (see
   page 19)
2 tablespoons coarse salt (kosher
   or pickling)
1 cup water
1 cup sugar

Peel the mangoes using a vegetable peeler, wash them, and transfer to a colander, giving it a few good shakes before sprinkling the salt over them. Set the colander in a larger bowl or over the sink to drain overnight. Bitter liquid will drain from the mangoes, much like from salted cucumbers.

The next morning rinse the mangoes under cold running water, shaking off any excess, then transfer them to a large, nonreactive glass bowl or a jar with a lid. Put the water and sugar in a saucepan and boil over medium-high heat, stirring constantly, until a thick syrup is formed. Pour the syrup over the mangoes, tossing to coat thoroughly, and cover the bowl. The mango pickles should be ready after 24 hours, but the longer the mangoes steep in the syrup, the better. Store the bowl or jar in the refrigerator, but do *not* seal.

The pickeled green mango and papaya are Filipino recipes from Madge Kho's (see also pages 89, 90, and 145). The papaya is excellent on its own, like a salad, or served along side grilled beef or meaty grilled fish, a true summer pleasure.

PICKLED GREEN MANGO

MAKES 2 CUPS

One 2-pound green or underripe
  mango (see page 20), pit
  removed, peeled and sliced thinly
  into sticks
¼ cup soy sauce
¼ sugar

Combine all the ingredients in a nonreactive glass or plastic bowl and stir to incorporate. Cover and let stand at room temperature overnight, then refrigerate for 3 to 4 days before eating.

ATCHARA
(Pickled Green Papaya)

MAKES 1 QUART

One 1-pound green papaya
  (see page 20), peeled, halved,
  and seeds removed
1¾ tablespoons coarse salt (kosher
  or pickling)
3 cups boiling water
½ cup distilled white vinegar
¼ cup sugar
4 to 6 spring onions, or 1 large leek,
  cut into quarters
1 carrot, coarsely shredded
1 small bell pepper or mild green
  chili, seeded and grated

In a large saucepan bring the water to a boil over high heat.

Grate the papaya into a large, nonreactive bowl, then sprinkle with 1 tablespoon of the salt and squeeze it into the papaya. Let stand for about 5 minutes. Pour the boiling water over the papaya and let stand for 10 minutes more.

Transfer the papaya to a colander, rinse under cold running water, and squeeze out all the excess liquid using the back of a spoon. Add the vinegar, sugar, and remaining ¾ teaspoon salt to the papaya and mix well. Transfer the papaya mixture to a saucepan over medium-high heat and bring to a boil.

Immediately turn off the heat and add the pepper, onion, and carrot, and mix well. Let cool and refrigerate for 12 hours or overnight. Consume within 2 weeks.

***P**ickling originated in ancient* Mesopotamia, near the Egypt of today. Kalustyan's Foods in Manhattan is a reliable source for Middle Eastern, as well as South Asian, food products. Arpiar Afarian is originally from Beirut, Lebanon, but he has been a New Yorker for many years. Arpiar creates most of the prepared foods sold at the store, including two kinds of pickles. He enjoys sharing his memories of Beirut—he refers to it as "the Paris of the Middle East"—and his love for its food.

Here he shares his recipes for colorful preserved lemons (in addition to the bright purple *lift,* or pickled turnip that is featured on page 91), which are both popular pickles throughout the Middle East and North Africa. This Moroccan recipe, which includes the subtle flavors of saffron and nigella is milder than Egyptian preserved lemons. "In Egypt, they might add a hot pepper or something else to spice things up," explains Arpiar. During pickling, the lemons absorb the salt from the brine and are faintly flavored by the spices.

Preserved lemons are a great source of vitamin C, but eat sparingly, considering the high sodium content of the brine. Preserved lemons are ideal when used in meat, fruit, and vegetable tagines, or stuffed in the cavity of a roast chicken. (Arpiar also mentions that these lemons are a popular snack with pregnant women!)

(continued on next page)

Arpiar Afarian with a display of preserved lemons at Kalustyan's foods. Photo courtesy of Lucy Norris.

KALUSTYAN'S PRESERVED LEMONS

8 small lemons (the size of Key limes), about 1½ pounds, halved, ends trimmed, tips and seeds removed
½ cup plus 2 tablespoons sea salt
⅓ cup fresh lemon juice (from 2 lemons)
1 teaspoon saffron
1 tablespoon nigella, or kalonji (see page 20)
1 tablespoon olive oil
1⅓ cups cold water

Sterilize the jar according to the directions on pages 12–14. Place the lemon halves in the hot jar, cut-side facing out. In a nonreactive bowl or pitcher, combine the salt, lemon juice, and water, stirring to combine. Pour the brine over lemons to cover, leaving 2 inches free at the top of the jar. Tightly screw on the lid and shake well. Add the olive oil, saffron, and nigella, screw on the lid again and shake well.

In the summer you can let the jar stand outside in a warm, sunny spot for 1 week, or in winter near a warm spot indoors (but do not let it cook), so that the lemons begin to ferment, then refrigerate. (If they are not refrigerated after a week, the lemons will become slimy.) It will take at least 3 weeks in the refrigerator before the lemons begin to lose their harsh bitterness and absorb the flavor of the brine instead. Refrigerated, the lemons will keep for up to 1 year.

M *& I International Foods* in Brighton Beach, Brooklyn, is probably the best-known source for Russian foods in New York. They make and sell extraordinarily flavorful and colorful pickles from all over Russian, Geogia, Ukraine, Latvia, and elsewhere in Eastern Europe.

Sophia Vinokurau provided a barrel of watermelon quarters to the NY Food Museum 2002 Pickle Day and people stood in line to taste a sample.

PICKLED WATERMELON QUARTERS WITH DILL

MAKES 4 GALLONS (SEE NOTE)

1 cup coarse salt (kosher or pickling)
1 cup sugar
1½ bunches celery, about 2 pounds, coarsely chopped
Fresh dill, about 1 pound, roots removed
4 tablespoons pickling spice
3 teaspoons crushed cayenne pepper
2 teaspoons distilled white vinegar
2 large garlic cloves, about 1 pound peeled and crushed ·
1 large watermelon, about 6 to 7 pounds, quartered
1½ gallons cold water

Combine all the ingredients except the watermelon in a large (4-gallon) bucket. Stir with a spoon until sugar and salt has dissolved, add the watermelon pieces. Cover and refrigerate for 1 week before serving.

Note: Most of us can't fit a 4-gallon bucket in our refrigerator, but this recipe is easily halved or quartered.

Sophia Vinokurau does not serve the sauerkraut along with these whole apples at M & I so the average person has no idea how the apples are pickles. Remarkably these apples stay crisp and sweet if eaten raw but they do have that tart briney flavor. Cooked in the sauerkraut it is fantastic served with pork sausage.

PICKLED WHOLE APPLES IN SAUERKRAUT

MAKES 1 GALLON

20 small to medium apples, left whole, any variety in season
½ gallon sauerkraut
½ pound fresh or frozen cranberries

Mix together all the ingredients in a large plastic bucket or pickling crock. Store in the refrigerator for 2 to 3 weeks before eating. Cover and refrigerated this will keep for 3 months. Serve cold with meat dishes.

This recipe was given to me by Mary Snead (for more from Mary see page 57). She says if fresh peaches aren't in season, she has also used canned. Serve these as a sweet and sour side dish to roast pork or game.

QUICK PICKLED PEACHES

MAKES 4 SMALL SERVINGS

¼ cup plus 2 tablespoons brown sugar, packed
½ cup cider vinegar
1½ cinnamon sticks
½ tablespoon whole cloves
5 to 6 fresh peaches (1 pound), halved, pitted, and peeled

In a large saucepan over medium heat, combine the brown sugar, vinegar, cinnamon sticks, and cloves; simmer for 5 minutes, stirring frequently, until a thick syrup forms. Add the peaches, raise the heat to medium-high, and boil for 5 minutes. Pour the peaches and syrup into a large nonreactive bowl and let stand until cool.

Cover the bowl with a plate, and refrigerate the peaches for 4 to 5 days before eating. They are best if consumed within 2 weeks.

$\mathcal{T}$his chutney is very close in texture and consistency to chunky peanut butter. It is nutty, spicy, and mellow-sweet and was given to me by Shihka Dalal (see also page 103). I enjoyed this chutney as a spread on toasted fresh bread, but it would make a great condiment for winter squash or sweet potato dishes too.

TAMARIND AND DATE CHUTNEY

MAKES 6 SMALL SERVINGS

3½ ounces (half of a 7-ounce block)
   tamarind paste (see page 21),
   diluted with hot water (see Note)
12 ounces fresh dates, pitted and
   chopped (yields ½ cup)
½ cup brown sugar
1 tablespoon cayenne pepper
½ cup sugar
¼ cup salt mix (1 tablespoon
   sea salt and 1 tablespoon coarse
   kosher salt)
1 teaspoon cumin

There are two methods for making this chutney. First, drain the tamarind paste in a fine-mesh sieve, using the back of a spoon to squeeze out the sour liquid; set aside the remaining pulp. Follow one of the two processes below to finish.

METHOD 1:
In a saucepan over high heat, combine the dates, water, sugar, 1 tablespoon salt mix, brown sugar, and tamarind pulp, and cook the mixture until it is the consistency of heavy cream, about 5 minutes. Remove from the heat, then add the cayenne, remaining salt, and cumin to taste, stirring to combine. Transfer the chutney to a jar and tightly screw on the lid.

Refrigerated, the chutney will last for up to 10 days.

METHOD 2:
Place all the ingredients in a blender and process until smooth. Add more sugar or salt to taste, transfer to a nonreactive bowl, and serve. The chutney will last for 2 to 3 days if covered and refrigerated.

Note: Tamarind paste is very thick. Dilute it in ½ to ¾ cup of hot water. This will make the paste less chunky, but take care that it does not have a watery consistency either.

***F*or a couple of years,** Jane Wilson Morton was the jam and pickle judge at the Long Island Fair (for more of Jane's recipes, see pages 86 and 104). In one day, she tasted more than two hundred different jellies, jams, and pickles! That was a bit much. Her stomach rebelled, so she told the fair organizers that she could judge one category or the other, but not both. Inspired by a batch that she judged at the fair, she created this recipe from her own taste-testing.

This recipe uses the flesh of fresh cantaloupe and spices from far-away places—allspice from Jamaica, cloves from the East Indies, and cinnamon from tropical Asia.

It's just not a summer picnic without pickles. Photo courtesy of Pickle Packers International.

SPICED PICKLED CANTALOUPE

MAKES 3 PINTS

2 firm, slightly underripe
cantaloupe, 2 pounds each
(yields 8 cups cubed)
1 quart plus 3 cups cold water
¼ cup coarse salt (kosher or
pickling)
2 to 3 cinnamon sticks, to taste
1½ tablespoons whole cloves
1½ tablespoons allspice berries
4 cups sugar
1 cup cider vinegar

Cut the melons in half, remove the seeds and rinds, and cut into 1-inch cubes. Transfer to a large, nonreactive bowl and set aside.

In another bowl, combine the 1 quart cold water with the salt, stirring to dissolve. Pour the salted water over the cantaloupe to cover, cover the bowl with a plate, and let it stand at room temperature for 3 hours.

When the cantaloupe is almost ready, put the 3 cups cold water in a large, nonreactive pot and bring to a rolling boil over high heat. Wrap the cinnamon, cloves, and allspice in a piece of cheesecloth and tie it up with a string. Add this spice bag, along wtih the sugar and vinegar, to the pot. Return the water to a boil, stirring frequently, until the sugar dissolves and a syrup has formed, about 10 minutes. Drain the cantaloupe, then add it to the syrup and boil for 10 minutes more. Cool completely, then cover and let stand overnight at room temperature.

The next morning, strain the syrup through a fine-mesh sieve into a large, nonreactive pot, reserving the cantaloupe pieces and syrup. Bring the syrup to a boil over medium-high heat and boil for 10 minutes. Add the cantaloupe to the syrup, return to a boil, then lower the heat and simmer gently for about 45 minutes, until the cantaloupe appears translucent.

In the meantime, sterilize the jars and lids according to the directions on page 000. Transfer the cantaloupe and syrup to the pint-sized jars leaving 1 inch free at the top and process in a hot-water bath for 10 to 15 minutes to seal (see pages 12–14). Let cool.

The sealed jars can be kept in a cupboard for up to 6 months. After opening, refrigerate and consume within 3 months.

CHAPTER SEVEN

Meat, Poultry, and Eggs

IN THE HIERARCHY OF FOOD THROUGHOUT HUMAN HISTORY, MEATS and poultry (in contrast to vegetable roots) have have long been associated with status, material wealth and prosperity. Who can imagine a special dinner or holiday feast without some form of meat—or meat-textured vegetable protein for vegetarians? Meat's association with wealth has long prevented it from being wasted by the old peasant classes all over the world; anything considered of great value had to be either used to its fullest or saved. Because of this, pickling or preserving meat has always been symbolically powerful.

Salt-curing, smoking, and drying are the most common ways to preserve meat and poultry. Although pickling seems ideal for meat (vinegars and spices act to mask strong or unpleasant odors), there are few recipes for pickled meat and poultry, with the exception of the fleshier, prime cuts of meat. I thought it was more interesting and appropriate to introduce you to the pickling traditions that emerged to use meats to their fullest. These are ways to stretch the whole hog past suppertime, so to speak.

This chapter is a brief introduction to pickled animal products, including eggs and offal, and the stories of the people who carry on these traditions. Included is a recipe for pickled pig's trotters (page 136) that shows how pickles can be used to help heal the body as well as nourish it.

———

*J*acqueline Newman has always been a curious eater. She remembers eating pickled duck tongues for the first time as a young teen at a big party thrown by one of her mother's friends in Chinatown. In fact, it was one of the first pickled Chinese foods she remembers eating. Admittedly, she says, she had no idea what they were the night she ate them, but being the inquisitive teen, she asked what she was eating and was amazed to find that a duck even had a tongue!

On the previous spread: At far left are Elsie Miller's Saloon Eggs (page 141).

This is probably one of the most fascinating recipes in this book. However, if you can't find (or tolerate the idea of) duck tongues, you can substitute shredded duck breast, or even chicken, with good results.

PICKLED DUCK TONGUES

MAKES 4 APPETIZER-SIZE SERVINGS

1 pound duck tongues; or 1 pound poultry breast, skinned and sliced into 1- by ⅛-inch strips
10 cups water
2 whole star anise
½ black cardamom pod, husk removed and discarded, smashed with the side of a cleaver
1 teaspoon Sichuan peppercorns
One 1-inch piece cinnamon bark, preferably Chinese
One 1-inch piece tangerine peel, soaked in water for 10 minutes, then minced
1 teaspoon sugar
1 teaspoon coarse salt (kosher or pickling)
2 tablespoons soy sauce thinned with 2 teaspoons water
3 tablespoons rice vinegar
2 tablespoons dark sesame oil

In a large pot, bring to a boil 8 cups of the water. Add the duck tongues (or strips of poultry breast) and boil for 5 minutes, then drain them in a colander. Rinse the meat under cold running water. Using your fingers, remove and discard the long thin cartilage from each tongue.

In a large saucepan, bring the remaining 2 cups water to a boil and add the star anise, cardamom, Sichuan peppercorns, cinnamon bark, tangerine peels, sugar, and salt; simmer for 3 minutes, then add the soy sauce and vinegar and stir. Remove the brine from heat, add the duck tongues (or breast strips), cover with a lid, and refrigerate the tongue mixture for 12 hours or overnight.

In the morning, drain the meat in a colander and transfer to a bowl. Add the sesame oil and stir well. Serve chilled as an appetizer. Refrigerated, this dish will stay fresh for about 1 week.

According to Alice Tse and Huikang Cheung, this dish is especially good for a woman after giving birth because it helps flush out impurities left in her body. Use the black syrupy vinegar found in Chinese groceries; you can add more sugar to suit your taste.

Alice believes that a good serving size of this "soup" should be no more than a half-cup of broth per day. Each serving, she explained, needs to have one pig trotter and one egg.

PIG TROTTERS IN GINGER AND BLACK VINEGAR

MAKES 4 MAIN COURSE SERVINGS

2½ cups black vinegar (see page 22)
4 large hard-boiled eggs, shelled
One 4-inch piece fresh ginger, peeled, washed, and minced
½ cup sugar, or to taste
2 front and 2 back pig trotters (about 4 pounds total)

Bring the black vinegar to a boil in a large, nonreactive pot. Add the sugar and stir to dissolve. Turn off the heat and add the boiled eggs and ginger. Cover the pot and let stand at room temperature for 24 hours.

In the meantime, put the pig trotters in a large pot, add water to cover, and boil for 20 minutes, or until the connective tissue breaks down or the meat and bone start to break up. Transfer the trotters to a large bowl lined with paper towels and let cool. Cover with a plate or lid and refrigerate for 12 hours or overnight.

The next day, bring the vinegar mixture, including the eggs to a boil again, add the pig trotters, and boil them for about 20 minutes. Turn off the heat, cover the pot, and let it stand overnight. The next day, heat the trotters by bringing the vinegar mixture to a boil before serving.

*S*ister May is a retired senior from China who regularly visits the Mott Street Senior Center in New York's Chinatown. She gave me this recipe for pickled chicken eggs on a notecard, handwritten in Cantonese.

This recipe and Good Mother's Salty Duck Eggs (page 139) are similar in their preparation, but used very differently. Sister May's Pickled Chicken Eggs have more salt and are brined much longer than the duck eggs; therefore, they are much stronger in taste. For most people, they are too strong to eat on their own and are harder to peel when soft boiled. But there are many ways in which these eggs are incorporated into other recipes. For example, these eggs would be delicious hard boiled and crumbled into congee, a traditional Chinese rice porridge that is frequently eaten for breakfast or, like chicken soup, as a comfort food when you are cold or sick. I have not included a recipe for congee here, but an excellent version can be found in *The Wisdom of the Chinese Kitchen* by Grace Young.

When considering their use in other dishes, please keep in mind that Sister May's eggs take 5 weeks to reach their full flavor.

SISTER MAY'S PICKLED CHICKEN EGGS

MAKES 1 DOZEN EGGS

1 dozen large, fresh chicken eggs
5 Chinese rice bowls or 4 cups
   coarse salt (kosher or pickling)
3 quarts water

Bring the water to a boil in a large, nonreactive pot, then add the salt and stir to dissolve. Remove from heat and allow the brine to cool to room temperature.

Carefully place the uncooked eggs in a pickling crock and pour the brine over them. To keep the eggs submerged, cover the crock with a plate small enough to fit inside it.

Store the crock in a cool, dark place for at least 5 weeks but no longer than 2 months. When you are ready to eat a pickled egg, remove it from the brine, rinse under cold running water, and cook the eggs as desired.

$\mathcal{L}$ynn Peemoeller, an American who has traveled through Thailand, learned this recipe from an elderly Thai woman. The salty duck egg pickle is also used in the recipe for Son-in-Law Eggs. Lynn shares her unusual travel story along with both recipes.

"I had to bend over to see Mae Dee, the Good Mother, and her tiny wrinkled square face. She was teaching me how to make salty duck eggs and she spoke Thai through a wide smile like she was singing a song. I had to struggle mightily to pick out the words I knew from my elementary vocabulary. Every day was a culinary adventure in the small village where I was staying in northern Thailand. Ingredients like water-buffalo hide, pink and purple foraged mushrooms, wild bamboo shoots, banana flowers, lime leaves, eels, and even spiders passed through the hands of village women at the market and ended up in the dishes that Mae Dee and others prepared for me.

"Salty duck eggs have a uniquely Asian taste originating from Chinese cuisine. I was very excited to learn that Mae Dee uses a traditional method of preparation. She takes fresh duck eggs straight from the nest and pickles them in a large, earthenware pot filled with salt brine for a minimum of a week before cooking them. The longer the eggs sit in the brine, the saltier they will be. Some people like to soak them for 1 month. As I understand it, this method was developed not only for taste but also as a system of preservation. Salting the egg in brine gives it a rich, dense texture when it is hard-boiled.

"These cooked eggs are widely eaten with Asian rice dishes like congee and the salted yolks are found in the moon cakes that celebrate the first autumn moon of the Chinese calendar. You can find brined, uncooked salty duck eggs in most Asian grocery stores, which you can buy as a shortcut, but I like the idea of making them myself. Fresh duck eggs are not as obscure as you may think: You can find them at most farmers' markets during the spring and summer."

Peemoeller explains, "The Thai mostly serve salty duck eggs simply cut in half and sprinkled with lime juice, chilies, cilantro, and fried shallots. However, I like the piquant recipe known as Son-in-Law Eggs. After the eggs are brined, they are boiled, peeled, fried, and served with a zesty sweet-and-sour tamarind sauce that cuts through the richness. This dish is called Son-in-Law Eggs, because it is a traditional wedding dish."

GOOD MOTHER'S SALTY DUCK EGGS

MAKES 1 DOZEN EGGS

4 quarts water
¾ cup coarse salt (kosher or
  pickling)
1 dozen fresh duck eggs

Bring the water to a boil in a large, nonreactive pot, then add the salt and stir to dissolve. Remove from the heat and cool to room temperature. Carefully place the uncooked eggs in a pickling crock and pour the brine over them. To keep the eggs submerged, cover the crock with a plate small enough to fit inside of it and place a weight on top of the plate.

Store the crock in a cool, dark place for 1 week. When you are ready to eat a pickled egg, remove it from the brine, rinse under cold running water, and cook as desired.

These eggs can replace any dish calling for soft or hard boiled eggs, including salads, porridges, and stews, but they are not very good scrambled.

Making Son-in-Law Eggs is a simple enough preparation, traditionally prepard by a new son-in-law for his new relatives. Sister May's Pickled Chicken Eggs (page 137) may also be used in this recipe, but they should only be brined for 1 week.

SON-IN-LAW EGGS

MAKES 6 SMALL SERVINGS

1 dozen Good Mother Salty Duck
  Eggs
1 cup peanut oil
½ cup tamarind concentrate or
  tamarind pulp diluted with water
1 cup water

½ cup palm sugar (see page 20) or
  light brown sugar
½ cup soy sauce
1 shallot, peeled and sliced
  (optional)
1 hot chili pepper, slices (optional)
½ cup chopped cilantro (optional)

(continued on next page)

Put the eggs in a large pot, add water to cover, and soft boil over medium heat, about 7 minutes. Carefully peel off the shells and prick the eggs with a fork, or they will explode.

Heat the peanut oil in a large skillet over high heat, add the whole eggs, and fry until crispy and golden, about 5 minutes. Transfer the eggs to paper towels to drain (reserve the hot peanut oil), then slice the eggs into quarters and arrange on a serving platter.

In a small saucepan combine the tamarind concentrate, water, palm sugar, and soy sauce and bring to a boil over medium heat. Set the sauce aside.

Fry the shallot in the reserved oil until crispy, but be careful not to burn them, then put on top of the eggs, along with the chilies and cilantro, if desired. Dribble sauce evenly over the eggs and serve hot.

*T*he practice of selling salty snacks at bars and pubs is an old gimmick to entice thirsty patrons to drink more beer and spirits. Pickled eggs, a previously popular accompaniment to beer, have slowly been replaced by salt potato chips. Nutritionally speaking, pickled eggs have the advantage over crispy fried potato chips, which are saturated with fat and have no nutriental value whatsoever.

This recipe comes from Steve Kennedy, a former student at the French Culinary Institute in New York, who passes it along with this bit of family history: "My great-grandparents owned a beer garden in Yorkville, the historically German Upper East Side of Manhattan, in the 1900s. Every day they would put out a free lunch for those who bought a beer (without the beer it was fifteen cents!). My great-grandmother, Elsie Miller, would make the sandwiches, salads, and pickles upstairs. My grandmother, then ten years old, would ride up and down in the dumbwaiter to deliver the victuals to the saloon downstairs. The spread always included pickled eggs."

These pickled saloon eggs are prettier and more delicious than any colored Easter egg and make a beautiful replacement for regular hard-boiled eggs. They remain white and yellow in the middle with a fuschia-colored skin on the outside.

ELSIE MILLER'S PICKLED SALOON EGGS

MAKES 1 QUART (STORE IN A 2-QUART JAR)

1 dozen large eggs, stored sideways
  in the carton for 24 hours to
  center the yolks
1½ quarts water, or more as needed
2½ cups distilled white vinegar
½ cup beet juice, made from boiling
  beets in water and reserving the
  cooking liquid
½ tablespoon whole cloves
½ tablespoon black peppercorns
2 tablespoons sugar
2½ small red chili peppers
1 to 2 blades of mace, to taste
  (see page 20)
1 whole star anise
1 bay leaf

Gently place the eggs in a large
pot and cover with at least 1½
quarts water. Bring to a boil over
high heat, then lower the heat and
simmer for 10 minutes. In the
meantime, sterilize the jar and lid
according to the directions on pages
12–14. Drain the eggs in a colander
and immediately crack the shells
and peel them under cold running
water.

Combine the vinegar, beet
juice, cloves, peppercorns, sugar,
chilies, mace, star anise, and bay
leaf in a pitcher. Stir with a long
spoon until the sugar is dissolved
to create a brine.

Pack the whole eggs in the
2-quart jar, cover with the brine,
and screw on the lid. (The brine
will not fill the jar, but using a
smaller container will not allow
enough room for the eggs to move
freely in the brine.)

Refrigerate for 5 days before
consuming, then serve with cold
cuts, cheese, and cold beer. This
recipe keep swell if refrigerated for
4 weeks; the inside of the eggs are
a mild white and yellow and the
flavor is delicate. At 2 months the
eggs are still edible but the brine
becomes very cloudy and the eggs
have a strong vinegar flavor.

CHAPTER EIGHT

Seafood and Fish

As the celebrated French gastronome Brillat-Savarin put it, "Fish is a *mezzo termine*" a middle course that agrees with almost every temperament. It is a compromise, neither too light nor too heavy for any appetite.

Unfortunately I am a late bloomer when it comes to appreciating seafood. I was not raised by the sea, so until I tasted my first truly fresh seafood, I had long associated it with a foul-smelling fishy odor and wondered how people could stomach the stuff.

Fish and shellfish are prized foods but extremely perishable, which for centuries has led humankind to search for ways to preserve it, at least for a short time, from spoiling. The ancient Romans used fish to their full extent when they made garum or fish liquid. This involved putting fish and shellfish entrails into barrels, salting them, and then leaving the mixture outside to ferment in the sun. When it was ready to be used, the liquid was strained and the garum was used to flavor many dishes.

Typically oily fish, like herring, is best for pickling, and a little citrus juice or vinegar goes a long way toward making even the fishiest fish more palatable. Some recipes in this chapter add the extra step of cooking the seafood over heat before it gets pickled. This dependably kills the bacteria present in the flesh, although the addition of acid (vinegar or citrus juice), plus a combination of spices, oils, sugar, or salt, also denatures or "cooks" raw seafood. Other approaches to seafood pickling include the recipe for salt codfish pickle (see page 147), in which an already preserved fish gets pickled.

On the previous spread: At far left is Pickled Shrimp (page 145).

Madge Kho got this recipe from a friend (see pages 89, 90, and 124 for Madge's other recipe contributions). The coriander seeds, slices of lemon, and vinegar make it quite delicious. Madge doesn't use salt, but I think it improves the flavor greatly.

PICKLED SHRIMP

MAKES 6 SMALL SERVINGS

1 pound medium to large shrimp,
  peeled and deveined
¼ cup distilled white vinegar
1 cup water
4 cloves garlic, peeled and crushed
3 tablespoons coriander seeds
2 tablespoons fennel seeds
1 tablespoon black peppercorns
1 teaspoon coarse sea salt
  (optional)
2 lemons, cut in half lengthwise
  then thinly sliced
2 large onions, thinly sliced into
  semicircles

Bring a large saucepan of water to a boil, and then add the shrimp and cook until they turn red and curl up, about 3 minutes. Drain the shrimp in a colander, then set aside in a large, nonreactive bowl to cool.

Put the vinegar and 1 cup water in another saucepan and bring to a boil, then stir in the garlic, coriander, fennel, peppercorns, and salt, if desired. Pour the brine over the shrimp to cover and toss to combine. Add the lemon and onion slices, toss to combine, and let the mixture cool.

Refrigerate the shrimp for 24 hours before eating. Serve chilled as a relish or appetizer. Refrigerated, the shrimp will keep for about 3 days.

*T*uhin *Dutta is the tandoori* master who cooks at Banjara restaurant in the East Village in New York City. I first heard about him when he presented a paper on the subject at an academic food conference of New York University hosted in the summer of 2002. Later, he contacted the NY Food Museum where I interviewed him about Indian pickling traditions for my original New York pickle stories project. (See his eggplant recipe on page 99.) It was a turning point in my research when I realized just how different cultures approach food preservation, especially pickling. Those familiar with the many regional differences in Indian cooking may recognize that the spices in this recipe are true to the Bihari and Bengal tastes. It is complex and spicy without the heat of chili. Tuhin admits he doesn't do much pickling—this is a recipe given to him by his mother and aunt.

MACHER ACHAAR
(Spicy Fish Pickle)

MAKES 1½ QUARTS, 6 SERVINGS

3½ tablespoons minced fresh ginger
3½ tablespoons minced garlic
1½ cups plus 1 tablespoon canola or vegetable oil
½ tablespoon water
1½ cups mustard oil (see page 20)
2 pounds small fish or shellfish, such as scallops, sardines, shrimp, or mackerel, cleaned, cut into bite-sized pieces, and patted dry with paper towels
1 tablespoon ajwain (see page 18)
1 tablespoon nigella or kolangi (see page 21)
¼ teaspoon asafoetida (see page 18)
½ teaspoon fenugreek seeds
1 onion, chopped

Cayenne pepper, to taste
1 tablespoon ground cumin
½ cup sugar or jaggery (see page 20)
1 to 1½ cups fresh lemon juice, to taste
Coarse salt (kosher or pickling), to taste

Using a mortar and pestle, make a paste out of the ginger, garlic, 1 tablespoon canola oil, and ½ tablespoon water. In a separate bowl, combine the mustard oil with the remaining 1½ cups canola oil and pour into a large skillet.

Heat the oil over medium heat, add the fish and fry until done, about 3 minutes. Using a slotted spatula, transfer the fish to a plate lined with paper towels and set aside.

146

Strain the hot oil through a fine-mesh sieve into a small bowl. Wipe the frying pan clean with a paper towel, reheat the strained oil over medium heat, then add the ajwain, nigella, asfoetida, and fenugreek, stirring until the spices begin to pop and crackle. Add the onion and cook until light brown, about 3 to 5 minutes, then add the ginger and garlic paste, stirring to combine. Cook until the mixture is brown but not burned and the raw aroma of the ginger and garlic has disappeared.

Lower the heat to medium and stir in the cayenne to taste and the cumin, sugar, and lemon juice and salt to taste; cook for 5 to 6 minutes, then remove from heat. While the mixture is still warm, add the fish and toss to combine, then set aside to cool. Transfer the mixture to a small earthenware crock with a tight lid and refrigerate for 3 to 4 days before serving.

he main ingredient in this dish, another Haitian recipe from Fabienne Volel, is salted codfish, better known as *bacalao* in the Latin community. This pickle is a salad, but it's more interesting than tuna salad. Eat it on a potato dinner roll like a sandwich. Another of Fabienne's favorite pickle recipes can be found on page 113.

CHIQUETAILLE DE MORUE
(Haitian Salt Cod Pickle)

MAKES 6 TO 8 SMALL SERVINGS

1 pound whole salted codfish
¾ cup vegetable oil or olive oil
3 scallions, chopped
4 medium onions, chopped
2 habanero chili peppers, seeded, cored, and chopped
1 garlic clove, minced
1 cup water
½ cup distilled white vinegar

Fill a large pot with water, add the codfish, and boil for 15 to 20 minutes to take away the excess salt. Transfer the fish to a fine-mesh sieve, let cool, then, using your hands, shred the fish into short strips and let drain for another 15 minutes.

Heat the oil in a large sauté pan over medium heat, add the scallions and sauté for about 30 seconds, stirring so they don't stick, then add the onions and let them sweat slightly, about 2 minutes. Add the

(continued on next page)

fish, habanero peppers, and crushed garlic and sauté them for about 3 minutes, until the fish has absorbed more liquid and become somewhat tender. *Do not let the onions become brown.*

Add the 1 cup water, raise the heat to medium-high, and boil for about 15 minutes, until the fish is firm but tender. Transfer the fish mixture to a large, nonreactive bowl, add the vinegar, and mix well.

Serve immediately. Leftovers will last for about 1 week if refrigerated.

Note: Haitians call habanero peppers piment bouk. *Habanero and Scotch bonnet are two of the hottest varieties of chilies, so please wear gloves when handling them, and don't allow anything that has been in contact with the peppers to touch your face or eyes.*

ℋenny **Helland spends much** of the year traveling back and forth between her home in Bergen, Norway, and New York City, where her husband is a professor at Columbia University. When she is in Manhattan, Henry works in the kitchen of the Norwegian Seaman's Church helping to feed a large community of transplanted Norwegians their favorite foods from home.

Her father and grandfather were both seamen. Although her father would be at sea for months, Henny remembers that he would always come home with lots of gifts. Besides clothes and household goods, one of the things he liked to bring home was pickles. Her mother didn't like to cook, but her father sometimes made pickled cauliflower, cucumbers, and carrots.

From *lutefisk,* a Scandinavian specialty made with unsalted dried cod, to pickled herring, fish is king in Norway, as in other Northern European countries. Pickled herring is eaten as a main dish, with potatoes on the side. Herring is an oily fish, so it is complemented by the spices and vinegar used to pickle it. No smorgasbord is complete without pickled herring. Henny says that this dish is normally served as an easy Christmas or summertime lunch. You just take the pickled herring out of the jar and serve it on a small plate with bread and butter. Salted herring can be purchased from a good fishmonger or kosher fish shop (see Sources, page 151–152).

GLASMESTERSILD

(Glacier's Pickled Herring)

4 large salted herrings, about
   3 pounds, or 8 fillets
4 cups plus 1¼ cups water
9 tablespoons distilled white
   vinegar
9 tablespoons sugar
1 to 2 medium-sized red onions,
   sliced, to taste
1 small leek, white part only, sliced
2 carrots, peeled and sliced
One 1-inch piece fresh horseradish
   root, peeled and cut into ½-inch
   cubes
25 white peppercorns
15 allspice berries
8 bay leaves

Under cold running water, clean the herrings, but if you are not using filets, leave the headless fish intact (don't remove the skin and bones). Place them in a large, nonreactive bowl and fill it with the 4 cups water enough to cover the herrings completely. Cover the bowl and store in the refrigerator for 24 hours to remove as much salt from the fish as possible.

The next day, in a small saucepan, combine the 1¼ cups water, vinegar, and sugar, bring to a boil, and stir until the sugar dissolves. Pour the syrup into a clean bowl, cover, and put into the refrigerator until chilled, about 1 hour.

Cut each herring into ¾-thick pieces. If you plan to store the pickled herring in a jar, sterilize a 2-quart jar and lid according to the directions on pages 12–14. In a mixing bowl, combine the onion, leek, carrots, horseradish, peppercorns, allspice berries, and bay leaves. In the sterilized jar or large glass bowl with a lid, layer equal amounts of the vegetable and spice mixture with the herring pieces until you've used up both.

Pour the syrup over the herring and vegetables and let sit for at least 30 minutes before serving. You can serve the pickled herring directly from the jar. If covered and refrigerated, it will stay fresh for up to 2 weeks.

Metric Conversion Charts

WEIGHT EQUIVALENTS

The metric weights given in this chart are not exact equivalents, but have been rounded up or down slightly to make measuring easier.

Avoirdupois	Metric
¼ oz	7 g
½ oz	15 g
1 oz	30 g
2 oz	60 g
3 oz	90 g
4 oz	115 g
5 oz	150 g
6 oz	175 g
7 oz	200 g
8 oz (½ lb)	225 g
9 oz	250 g
10 oz	300 g
11 oz	325 g
12 oz	350 g
13 oz	375 g
14 oz	400 g
15 oz	425 g
16 oz (1 lb)	450 g
1½ lb	750 g
2 lb	900 g
2¼ lb	1 kg
3 lb	1.4 kg
4 lb	1.8 kg

VOLUME EQUIVALENTS

These are not exact equivalents for American cups and spoons, but have been rounded up or down slightly to make measuring easier.

American	Metric	Imperial
¼ t	1.2 ml	
½ t	2.5 ml	
1 t	5.0 ml	
½ T (1.5 t)	7.5 ml	
1 T (3 t)	15 ml	
¼ cup (4 T)	60 ml	2 fl oz
⅓ cup (5 T)	75 ml	2½ fl oz
½ cup (8 T)	125 ml	4 fl oz
⅔ cup (10 T)	150 ml	5 fl oz
¾ cup (12 T)	175 ml	6 fl oz
1 cup (16 T)	250 ml	8 fl oz
1¼ cups	300 ml	10 fl oz (½ pt)
1½ cups	350 ml	12 fl oz
2 cups (1 pint)	500 ml	16 fl oz
2½ cups	625 ml	20 fl oz (1 pt)
1 quart	1 liter	32 fl oz

OVEN TEMPERATURE EQUIVALENTS

Oven Mark	F	C	Gas
Very cool	250-275	130-140	½-1
Cool	300	150	2
Warm	325	170	3
Moderate	350	180	4
Moderately hot	375	190	5
Hot	400	200	6
	425	220	7
Very hot	450	230	8
	475	250	9

Sources

GENERAL INFORMATION
PICKLE PACKERS INTERNATIONAL, INC.
P.O. Box 606
One Pickle and Pepper Plaza
St. Charles, IL 60174
www.ilovepickles.com
The trade association for the pickled vegetable industry provides a wealth of information about pickles. Their web site includes material for educators, recipes, and an alphabetical listing of international pickle brands with contact information.

WWW.PICKLENET.COM
This U.K.–based on-line information service offers information on pickling, a recipe forum, and a pickling expert who answers questions posted via e-mail. A shopping service provides links to British companies for prepared foods and an attractive array of canning jars.

EQUIPMENT
ALLTRISTA CONSUMER PRODUCTS CO.
Consumer Affairs
P.O. Box 2729
Muncie, IN 47307-0729
www.homecanning.com
Questions about canning:
Toll free: 1 (800) 240-3340
On-line orders: 1 (800) 392-2575
Alltrista is the maker of Ball and Kerr jars in the U.S. and Bernadin jars in Canada. Their extensive web site (serving the U.S. and Canada) offers detailed information related to home canning. Their complete product line is available for on-line order.

HOME CANNING SUPPLY & SPECIALTIES
P.O. Box 1158-WW
Ramona, CA 92065
Tel: (760) 788-0520
Fax: (760) 789-4745
To order or request a catalog:
1 (800) 354-4070 or
www.homecanningsupply.com
A complete line of products for home food preservation, including pickling crocks, canning jars, pickling salt and lime.

THE HOUSE OF RICE STORE
3221 N. Hayden Road
Scottsdale, AZ 85251
Toll free: 1(877) 469-1718
Fax: (480) 947-0889
www.houserice.com
Sells a Japanese pickle press, mandoline, and other Asian cooking equipment.

INGREDIENTS AND SPICES
FAMOUS FOODS
1595 Kingsway
Vancouver, BC V5N 2R8 Canada
Tel: (604) 872-3019
Large selection of spices and salts.

KALUSTYAN'S
123 Lexington Avenue
New York, New York 10016
Tel: (212) 685-3451
www.kalustyans.com
Importers, exporters, and distributors of Indian and Middle Eastern gourmet foods. Many of the spices mentioned in this book can be ordered from their website.

NORDIC DELICACIES
6909 Third Avenue
Brooklyn, New York 11209
Tel: (718) 748-1874
www.nordicdeli.com
All manner of Scandanavian foods including salted herring.

PARS INTERNATIONAL
1801 Lonsdale Avenue
North Vancouver, BC V7M 2J8, Canada
Tel: (604) 988-3515
Fax: (604) 985-0206
International bulk spices.

PENZEYS SPICES
19300 Janacek Court
P.O. Box 924
Brookfield, WI 53008-0924
Toll free: 1(800) 741-7787
Fax: (262) 785-7678
www.penzeys.com
A bounty of spices, salts, and dried herbs.

PRECISION FOOD
4975 West Main Street, Highway 6 West
P.O. Box 2067
Tupela, MS 38001
Tel: (662) 842-6790
Pickling lime, salt, and citric acid.

SAHADI'S FINE FOODS
187 Atlantic Avenue
Brooklyn, New York 11235
Tel: (718) 624-4550
www.sahadis.com
Importers, exporters, and distributors
of Indian and Middle Eastern gourmet foods.

PREPARED FOODS AND PICKLES
*Many of these businesses have provided recipes,
stories, or information for this book.*

GOURMET GARDENS
P.O. Box 427, Route 5
Rusk, TX 75785
Tel: (903) 683-5726
www.gourmet-gardens.com
Hand-packed FDA approved pickles,
preserves, syrups, and salsas.

GUSS' PICKLES
85-87 Orchard Street
New York, NY 10002
Tel: (516) 569-0909
Kosher pickles from the barrel
and horseradish.

M&I INTERNATIONAL FOODS
249 Brighton Beach Avenue
Brooklyn, New York 11235
Tel: (718) 615-1011
Russian, Ukrainian, Latvian, and Georgian specialty foods.

MOUNT OLIVE PICKLE COMPANY
Corner of Cucumber & Vine
P.O. Box 609
Mount Olive, NC 28365
Toll free (800) 672-5041
Tel: (919) 658-2535
Fax: (919) 658-6296
The largest privately held pickle
company in the U.S.

PAT'S PEA PATCH
Stalls 129-141, Dallas Farmers Market
1010 S. Pearl Expressway
Dallas, TX 75201
Tel: (214) 748-6505
Family-run farm-fresh produce, pickles, and
preserves. Hand-packed by Gourmet Gardens.

THE PICKLE PEOPLE
103–129 Woodfield Road
West Hempstead, NY 11552
Tel: (516) 481-5350
Produces pickle products based on family
recipes, sold from a concession stand inside
Western Beef and at street fairs.

RALPH SECHLER & SON, INC.
5686 SR 1,
St. Joe, IN 46785
Toll-free 1(800) 332-5461
Tel: (260) 337-5461
Fax: (260) 337-5771
www.gourmetpickles.com
Thirty-nine varieties of pickles made
by traditional methods.

UNITED PICKLE PRODUCTS
4366 Park Avenue
Bronx, NY 10457
Tel: (718) 933-6060
Fax: (718) 367-8522
Wholesale pickle products sold
worldwide.

WOO LAE OAK RESTAURANT
148 Mercer Street
New York, NY 10012
Tel: (212) 925-8200
Upscale Korean restaurant with
a French twist.

STRUB BROTHERS LTD.
100 Roy Boulevard
Brantford, Ontario N3R 7K2 Canada
Toll free: 1(800) 38-STRUB/(387-8782)
A wide range of traditional pickles
and flavors.

UNIQUE FOODS LTD.
51-A Caladari Road, Suite 12
Concord, Ontario L4K 4G3 Canada
Tel: (905) 761-6906
Fax: (905) 761-6907
www.unique-foods.com
Indian food purveyor with a pickle line that
includes mango pickles; available in fine food
stores across Canada.

A Brief Guide to North American Annual Pickle Festivals

NEW YORK FOOD MUSEUM INTERNATIONAL PICKLE DAY

Held annually in autumn.
NY Food Museum
P.O. Box 222, Prince Street Station
New York, NY 10012
Tel: (212) 966-0191
NYFoodMuse@aol.com
www.nyfoodmuseum.org.

ATKINS PICKLE FEST

Held annually in May.
People for a Better Atkins
P.O. Box 474
Atkins, AR 72823
Tel: (501) 641-7210.

BERRIEN SPRINGS SUMMER AND CHRISTMAS PICKLE FESTIVAL

P.O. Box 30
Berrien Springs, MI 49103
Tel: (616) 449-2910
E-mail clvoyt@ameritech.net

DILLSBURG PICKLEFEST

Held annually in autumn.
Maple Shade Barn
Greenbrier Road & Harrisburg Pike
Dillsburg, PA 17019
E-mail maneman@igate.com
www.localpickle.com

GREENLAWN—CENTERPORT HISTORICAL SOCIETY PICKLE FESTIVAL

Greenlawn Centerport Historical Assoc.
P.O. Box 354
Greenlawn, NY 11740
Tel: (631) 754-1180
E-mail GCHA-Info@usa.net

MT. OLIVE PICKLEFEST

Mount Olive Airport
123 North Center
Mt. Olive, NC 28365
Tel: (919) 658-3113
E-mail moacc@coastalnet.com
www.ncpicklefest.org

ROSENDALE'S INTERNATIONAL PICKLE FESTIVAL

Held annually in November.
Rosendale Recreation Center
Route 32
Rosendale, NY, 12472
Tel: (845) 658-9649
E-mail info@picklefest.com
http://picklefest.com

ST. JOE PICKLE FEST

Held annually in autumn.
County Road 60 & State Road 1
St. Joe, IN 46785
Tel: (260) 337-5470
http://stjoepickle.com

GOOD FOOD FESTIVAL & MARKET

Held annually in May.
Mississauga, Ontario Canada
Tel: (416) 766-2084

Bibliography

Brennan, Jennifer. *The Cuisines of Asia.* New York: St. Martin's/Marck, 1984.

Brillat-Savarin, Jean Anthelme. *The Physiology of Taste or Meditations on Transcendental Gastronomy.* Washington D.C.: Counterpoint, 2000. Translation copyright Heritage Press, 1949.

Davidson, Alan. *The Oxford Companion to Food.* Oxford: Oxford University Press, 1999.

Flower, Barbara and Elizabeth Rosenbaum. *The Roman Cookery Book: A Critical Translation of the Art of Cooking by Apicius.* London: George G.Harrap & Co.

Hilliard, Sam. From *Hogmeat and Hoecake: Food Supply in the Old South, 1840-1860: All Kinds of Good Rations,* 1972 . Carbondale: Southern Illinois University Press.

Kalcik, Susan. "The Performance of Group Identity" in *Ethnic and Regional Foodways in the United States*, edited by Linda Keller Brown and Kay Mussel. Knoxville: University of Tennessee Press, 1984.

Rosenberger, Bernard. "Arab Cuisine and Its Contribution to European Cultures" in *A Culinary History of Food*, edited by Jean-Louis Flandrain and Massimo Montanari. New York: Columbia University Press, 1999.

Shephard, Sue. *Pickled, Potted, and Canned: The Story of Food Preserving.* London: Headline, 2000.

Spivey, Diane M. *The Peppers, Crackling, and Knots of Wool Cookbook: The Global Migration of African Cuisine,* 1999. New York: State University of New York Press.

Ziedrich, Linda. *The Joy of Pickling.* Boston: Harvard Common Press, 1998.

NY Food Museum

The NY Food Museum is a non-profit organization dedicated to encouraging people to think about the food they eat. The museum sponsored the great research and outreach that laid the groundwork for *Pickled*, and we hope to take that creativity and sense of adventure into all our future activities. Come with us as we create exhibits, events, videos and get-togethers celebrating food, ethnic diversity, community traditions and the history of New York. Membership gets you 6 great newsletters about New York's food traditions, special mailings and a free gift.

ANNUAL MEMBERSHIP FORM

Name:_____

Address:_____

City, State, Zip:_____

Phone: _____   Email:_____

Make your $50 check out to: NY Food Museum and send it with a photocopy of this form to: NY Food Museum, PO Box 222, New York, NY 10012.

Visit our website at www.nyfoodmuseum.org for online exhibits and museum news. The NY Food Museum is a 501c(3) organization. Contributions are tax-deductible to the fullest extent of the law.

ACKNOWLEDGMENTS

First, allow me to pay tribute to Nancy Ralph, the director of the New York Food Museum (NYFM). Nancy politely but cautiously handled my early enthusiasm as she does any potential volunteer, by starting me on low-risk tasks. Eventually (because I never went away) the small tasks accumulated and I became part of the group. Not quite a full year later, I offered to write a book. Thankfully, Nancy Ralph not only supported the project's metamorphosis, but encouraged me to develop it by offering her time, creativity, and helpful criticism along the way. I can't thank her enough.

I also want to extend a heart felt thanks to Dana Bowen, a talented food writer and reporter, who helped research and interview some of the contributors who appear in this book. Dana tested recipes, took photographs, and generally did a lot of work that helped me directly and indirectly while she was writing her own book!

A special thanks to the NYFM board: Suzanne Wasserman, Alexandra Leaf, Gail Johnson, and Lynn Loflin. This "think tank" of super-creative individuals gave me the supportive green light to "go for it."

Humble thanks to Tara Bahrampour of the *New York Times*, who not only wrote a great article in the City section about my research, but became a pickle fan. In addition, thanks to former Mayor Ed Koch for doing a fine job as celebrity pickle taster for her article. To Midge Elias and the New York Restaurant School, thanks for allowing us into one of the school's kitchens during the early phase of recipe testing. We had a great day!

Thanks to the editorial staff at Stewart, Tabori & Chang for your help and Sarah Scheffel for her eagle-eye queries. It was very helpful. Thank you Marisa Bulzone, my editor and fellow pickle fan. Your sincerity and understanding of my vision was constant throughout our work together and I appreciate you so much for that. Thanks to combined artistic talents of Elizabeth Watt and Nina Barnett, the book is more beautiful than I ever imagined. Thanks to Grace Young, whose own lovely book inspired me to contact her agent because I had only wished my book could be half as special. Thanks Martha Kaplan for guiding me through the re-write(s) of the original proposal and for also being a good-humored pickle fan.

Cheers to Shirley Fu and John Hsu for translating handwritten Chinese recipes and to Min-Jung Nam for e-mailing me from Korea on her summer vacation to demystify key Korean ingredients.

Thanks to the faculty and staff at New York University's Department of Nutrition and Food Studies, especially Marion Nestle, Jennifer Schiff-Berg, and Trish Lobenfeld for their utmost support throughout this project.

A most profound thank-you goes to Dean Frances White and the Gallatin School of Individualized Study. I want to especially thank my teachers Ann Axtmann, Julie Malnig, Pat Rock, and Jean Graybeal providing me a "higher education" than I ever hoped for in an undergraduate program.

Thanks to my partner Jason, and to Willie and Georgia, who all earn T-shirts for surviving the smells from the recipe testing and for enduring my excitement about pickles. Thanks to Annette Wenzel for listening to my worries but always believing that this book would be someday be published (that meant so much to me). Thanks to my parents Linda Almes and Dahrell Norris, for their support and encouragement along the way. And to Aunt Katie and Aunt Judith Lowther along with my parents for being "sources of the knowledge" in their own right. Thanks to my friend Stephanie Gould for her good humor and constant praise for the "pickle lady."

To my friends and those who helped along the way on this project, thanks especially to Nif Minnick, Tessa Thompson, Jean Hogan, Annie Hauck-Lawson, Andrea Dunn, Priscilla Ferguson, Greg Masters, Joe Wehry, Marc Burch, Peter Erskine, Jon Deutsch, Emily Rubin, and Corinna Hawkes.

And to my coworkers at The Center for Teaching Excellence for their patience while I switched hats from co-worker to student to author.

Thanks to these businesses and organizations for their support of my own and NYFM efforts to collect and celebrate historic food ways and cultural diversity and for allowing us to eat their inventory, take photographs, bug them about their businesses, and even in some cases record on-site interviews: United Pickle, Kalustyan's, Guss' Pickles, Asia Society, Pickle People, Russ and Daughters', Rosendale Picklefest, Dean's Pickles, Norwegian Seaman's Church, Sahadi's, Hanareum, Pat's Pea Patch, Gourmet Gardens, Sunshine Pickles, Pickle Packers Association, M&I International Foods, and Mott Street Senior Center.

And last but certainly not least, this book could not have been complete without the wonderful recipes and/or personal stories of friends and contributors: Arpiar Afarian, Fabienne Volel, Evelyn Cassidy, Gwinda Anthony, Henny Helland, Huikuang Cheung, Alice Tse, Jacqueline Newman, Tim Baker, Evelyn Cassidy, Dr. Robert Blake, Barbara Berdon, Michelle Gilbert, Anne-Lacy Boswell, Jane Hauck, Alana Lawson, Jane Maharam, Jane Wilson Morton, Jerilyn Gates, Eddie and Lee Ann Jacobian, Luyben Tachev, Lynn Peemollier, Madge Kho, Mary Katherine Moore, Mary Snead, Michael Born, Pat Sherlock, Renuka Potluri, Salvatore Agrogento and Arlyn Blake, Shihka Dalal, Sister May, Sol Weinberg, Sophia Vinokurav, Steve Kennedy, Theresa and Julian Ezstergalyos, Tim Shaw, Tina Yam, Tuhin Dutta, Steve Leibowitz, Vladimir and Yelena Groysman, Young S. Choi, Sophie and Françoise Raimbault, Nikki Rossi, Barbara Bradshaw, and Theresa Rose.

Readers may find some favorite recipes missing from this collection. There are many famous pickles in the world and I am only sorry I couldn't include them all.

INDEX